Higher ENGLISH

LANGUAGE SKILLS

for CfE

ANSWERS AND MARKING SCHEMES

Mary M. Firth and Andrew G. Ralston

SCOTTISH EXAMINATION MATERIALS

HODDER GIBSON
AN HACHETTE UK COMPANY

The Publishers would like to thank the following for permission to reproduce copyright material:

Photo credits Chapter opener image reproduced on pages 1, 3, 4, 5, 7, 8, 12, 13, 15, 19, 21, 23, 25, 27, 29, 34, 40, 43, 47, 48, 49, 50 and 52 © Rido – Fotolia.com.

Acknowledgements

Every effort has been made to trace all copyright holders, but if any have been inadvertently overlooked the Publishers will be pleased to make the necessary arrangements at the first opportunity.

Although every effort has been made to ensure that website addresses are correct at time of going to press, Hodder Gibson cannot be held responsible for the content of any website mentioned in this book. It is sometimes possible to find a relocated web page by typing in the address of the home page for a website in the URL window of your browser.

Hachette UK's policy is to use papers that are natural, renewable and recyclable products and made from wood grown in sustainable forests. The logging and manufacturing processes are expected to conform to the environmental regulations of the country of origin.

Orders: please contact Bookpoint Ltd, 130 Park Drive, Abingdon, Oxon OX14 4SE. Telephone: (44) 01235 827720; Fax: (44) 01235 400454. Lines are open 9:00–5:00, Monday to Saturday, with a 24-hour message answering service. Visit our website at www.hoddereducation.co.uk. Hodder Gibson can be contacted direct on: Tel: 0141 848 1609; Fax: 0141 889 6315; email: hoddergibson@hodder.co.uk

© Mary M. Firth, Andrew G. Ralston 2015
First published in 2015 by
Hodder Gibson, an imprint of Hodder Education,
An Hachette UK Company,
2a Christie Street
Paisley PA1 1NB

Impression number	5 4 3 2
Year	2019 2018 2017 2016 2015

Cover photo © Rido – Fotolia.com
Illustrations by Integra Software Services Pvt. Ltd.
Typeset in 12/14.5pt Minion Regular by Integra Software Services Pvt. Ltd., Pondicherry, India
Printed in the UK
A catalogue record for this title is available from the British Library.
ISBN: 978 1 471 84441 6

CONTENTS

I UNDERSTANDING THE MEANING

USING YOUR OWN WORDS

For practice (page 3)

1. *Identify four of the beliefs held about the island of Eynhallow that contributed to its supernatural reputation.* (**4 marks**)
Eynhallow was believed to disappear and reappear (**1 mark**); people believed that grain would bleed if they cut it there at night (**1 mark**); cats, rats and mice were not thought to survive on the island (**1 mark**); people believed laying down earth from the island kept vermin away from stacks or houses (**1 mark**).

For practice (page 3)

2. a) *Explain the nature of agricultural work during the author's childhood.* (**2 marks**)
Work was extremely hard and physically demanding.
Work was done by hand without the help of machines.
It involved frustrating waits for good weather and plants to grow.
(Any two; 1 mark for each.)

   b) *Identify three further aspects of village life at that time.* (**3 marks**)
Villages were very isolated.
Contact was made on foot or by horse and cart.
People rarely visited, and only if the visit was strictly essential.
The pace of life was very slow, with no motorised vehicles.
(Any three; 1 mark for each.)

For practice (page 3)

3. *Identify four reasons why the author found Barcelona astonishing.* (**4 marks**)
The workers were in control of the city, something the author had never experienced before.
All large buildings were covered in red flags or the anarchists' own flag.
The walls were all covered in graffiti – hammer and sickle emblems and the initials of the political parties in power.
The churches were all destroyed.
The sacred contents of the churches had been burnt.
(Any four; 1 mark for each.)

For practice (page 4)

4. a) *In your own words, identify three types of activities that have always been considered to be 'art'.* (**3 marks**)
   Constructing pieces of architecture (places of worship or places to live in).
   Painting, drawing, carving.
   Producing tapestry/cloth that incorporates designs.

   b) *Identify three things that the writer says would only in recent times be considered 'art'.* (**3 marks**)
   Well-designed, expensive personal possessions.
   Items exhibited in museums and galleries.
   Decorative objects for the home.

For practice (page 4)

5. a) *Explain what was noteworthy about the winter of 1542.* (**2 marks**)
   It was very severe. (**1 mark**) The weather was stormy and there was deep snow and hard frost. (**1 mark**)

   b) *In your own words, identify five political problems that were facing Scotland.* (**5 marks**)
   Scotland had just been severely beaten by England at the battle of Solway Moss.
   Many of the most eminent Scottish noblemen had been killed at Solway Moss, after their numbers had already been seriously depleted at the battle of Flodden only a generation earlier.
   Many other important Scottish noblemen were prisoners of the English.
   Those surviving noblemen in Scotland had a tendency to quarrel among themselves, and were only interested in personal gain.
   The Scottish Church, which was still Catholic, was riven by the struggle between those who wished to reform the Church from within and those who wished to follow the English example and break away from Rome.
   The King was dying and unwilling or unable to confront the problems.
   (*Any five, sufficiently detailed; 1 mark per point.*)

LINK QUESTIONS

For practice (page 7)

1. *Show how the highlighted sentence acts as a link in the argument.* (**3 marks**)
   'But' indicates a contrast will follow. (**1 mark**) The phrase 'illicit grandeurs of her forebears' refers back to the idea of the mother's aristocratic ancestors at 'the Castle', and her being related to the noblemen who murdered Edward II (**1 mark**); the phrase 'quite ordinary poverty' links in the idea of his mother's simple and hard-up living conditions, which are then listed in detail (**1 mark**).

For practice (page 7)

2. *Show how the first sentence of the second paragraph acts as a link in the argument.* (**3 marks**)
   'However' points to a change in fortune. (**1 mark**) The phrase 'the position' refers to the stance the beggar had occupied at the end of the drive by the gates (**1 mark**); 'brought the old man little benefit' introduces in an understated way the information that the old man became too weak to beg, and eventually died of exposure after a snowfall (**1 mark**).

For practice (page 8)

3. *Show how the highlighted sentence acts as a link in the argument.* (**2 marks**)
   The phrase 'the appearance' links back to the previous paragraph, which was a list of the features of the Queen's beauty (**1 mark**); the phrase 'the character of Mary Stuart' introduces a description of her inner qualities, such as her intellect and personality (**1 mark**).

For practice (page 8)

4. *Demonstrate that the highlighted sentence performs a linking function between the two paragraphs.* (**2 marks**)
   The phrase 'all these qualities' refers back to the list of Einstein's eccentricities, such as wearing no socks (*1 mark*); 'would still not have been sufficient' leads on to what was necessary to make him an international celebrity – 'the missing ingredient' – which was the extreme difficulty of his theory (**1 mark**).

For practice (page 8)

5. *Show how the highlighted phrase relates to what has gone before it and introduces a new idea to be developed in the remainder of the paragraph.* (**2 marks**)
   The word 'vast' refers back to the very large numbers of people working in service (**1 mark**); the word 'heterogeneous', which means 'of many different kinds', leads into the explanation of the huge variety of types of servant (**1 mark**).

For practice (page 9)

6. *Show how the highlighted sentence acts as a link.* (**2 marks**)
   The phrase 'the years as a golden boy' refers back to the description of Alastair's successful school career (**1 mark**); the phrase 'made a sad contrast' leads up to the list of disasters that overtook him later, at university (**1 mark**).

DENOTATION AND CONNOTATION

For practice (page 10)

The following pairs of words have similar denotations but different connotations, as at least one of the pair is a metaphor. Explain what the connotations are, and how they are likely to affect the mood and/or tone of the writing in which they are used:

a) *journey/pilgrimage*

'Journey' means a physical act of travelling. As such, the word is emotionally neutral. It is now frequently used as a metaphor to mean making progress in some endeavour. As such it can have emotive force.

'Pilgrimage' has religious connotations. Originally meaning a journey made as a religious pledge, it is also used to mean a journey to somewhere of special (emotional) significance to the traveller.

b) *campaign/crusade*

A 'campaign' is a prolonged plan of action. It has military connotations. It is now frequently used in the worlds of politics and advertising.

The word 'crusade' is derived from the Latin for 'cross', and originally referred to wars aiming to establish Christianity over Islam in Turkey and Palestine. Having strong religious connotations, it is now used metaphorically to mean any prolonged plan of action with strongly idealistic motives.

c) *enquiry/probe*

'Enquiry' is a neutral word meaning an investigation into something.

A 'probe' is a thin pointed instrument used by doctors or dentists to examine the body. Metaphorically it means a very intensive, even intrusive, enquiry into something.

d) *flood/tsunami*

A 'flood' means a large invasion of water. It is often used metaphorically to mean an overwhelming quantity of something. It may have destructive connotations.

A 'tsunami' is a colossal, very destructive tidal wave. It is also used as a metaphor, but with much stronger, more devastating connotations than 'flood'. Its use has become more common since the tsunami in Thailand on Boxing Day 2004 claimed over a quarter of a million lives.

e) *surrounded/besieged*

'Surrounded' is a generally neutral word meaning having something/someone on all sides. Depending on context, it might have connotations of entrapment.

'Besieged' has military connotations, meaning being encircled and trapped by enemy troops. It is a more emotive word than 'surrounded' when used metaphorically, with suggestions of being overwhelmed by aggressive opponents.

SHADES OF MEANING

For practice (page 12)

1. *Here is a selection of ten words connected with the idea of liveliness.*
   a) *Tick the correct box according to whether you think the word has a positive or negative effect.*
   b) *Comment on any particular connotations you associate with each word.*

	Positive	Negative	Might be positive *or* negative	What you associate with the word
vigorous	✓			Often used to describe plants that grow well.
dynamic	✓			Connected with 'dynamo', hence having the energy of a machine.
rumbustious			✓	Used of children who are too lively; word has slightly comic overtones so is often used indulgently.
rowdy		✓		Suggests unpleasant, loud, bad behaviour.
unruly		✓		Less negative than 'rowdy', but suggests out-of-control behaviour.
boisterous			✓	Associated with children, who are over-active but in an amusing way.
wild			✓	Suggests being out of control. This might be seen as exciting.
hyperactive			✓	A word with medical overtones; used of children but suggesting excessive behaviour that they cannot help.
lively	✓			Can have mental as well as physical associations to do with attitude.
energetic	✓			Implies being active in a positive, achieving way.

2. *Explain the shades of meaning between the following pairs of words.*

a) *childlike/childish*

Both words relate to behaving in a way associated with a very young person. 'Childlike' means 'like a child' and has generally neutral or slightly positive connotations of innocence. 'Childish' has negative connotations as it suggests the person is acting in an immature manner.

b) *inquisitive/nosy*

'Inquisitive' means interested in finding things out; it is generally a neutral term but may suggest an inclination to pry. 'Nosy' is negative, implying an uncalled for or intrusive interest in things that are no concern of the enquirer.

c) *question/interrogate*

'Question' is largely neutral, meaning to ask for information. 'Interrogate' has aggressive overtones, implying repeated questioning in order to extract information that the person does not want to give, possibly with threats.

d) *shrewd/calculating*

'Shrewd' is a generally positive term, meaning someone is clever and perceptive, not easily fooled. 'Calculating' is similar, but more negative, implying thinking in a selfish way, trying to fool others and gain advantage over them.

e) *gloomy/sullen*

'Gloomy' means unhappy, depressed or pessimistic. 'Sullen' is more negative, meaning unhappy, but with an overtone of sulkiness and having a bad attitude to other people.

(Answers will vary.)

For practice (page 13)

3. *Comment on the connotations of the highlighted word(s) in each of the examples, and how they contribute to the writer's meaning.*

a) 'Soared' has connotations of a rocket or bird going vertically upwards very fast. It suggests a sudden huge increase in sales.

b) 'Antiquated' has connotations of antiques, or things dug up by an archaeologist. It suggests the car was extraordinarily old, from a different age.

c) 'Incandescent' suggests something white hot. This indicates the extreme level of anger, as people get 'heated' and their faces turn red or even pale when they are very angry.

d) 'Hissed' suggests a snake, which has connotations of treachery and poison. It implies the sister hates in a venomous and implacable way.

e) 'Clamp' is a metal device to stop movement, like a wheel clamp on a vehicle. This suggests the police were effective in stopping the gang's activities.

f) 'Kick-start' is a metaphor; the image is of starting a motorcycle by forcing down a foot-lever. The bike can then roar off very fast. This suggests the tax breaks were effective in getting the mining started without delay.

g) A 'cocoon' is the smooth protective case round an insect pupa as it develops into an adult form. It implies the Lords was a safe, comfortable and protected environment where people can perhaps remain inert.

h) 'Dose' is a metaphor, and implies a measured amount of medicine. This suggests a reasonable amount of sunshine can be beneficial in many ways.

i) 'Bake' is to cook bread or cake in a hot oven. This suggests the heat in California is dry and excessive.

j) 'Soldier on' means to behave like a soldier: to battle on against adversity. This implies fighting bravely against illness instead of giving in.

SUMMARISING THE MAIN POINTS

For practice (page 14)

The two extracts are from the same article. Summarise the main point(s) made in each paragraph.

a) The benefits of biofuels include being carbon neutral, replaceable, plentiful and easily grown.

b) Biofuels are likely to be important in the future and may well produce savings. The term covers many different types of product, however, and factors like the way these are grown and their potential to cause pollution must be taken into account as well as the financial benefits.

For practice (page 15)

Summarise the three objections to biofuels put forward by the writer in the extract. (**3 marks**)

Three objections are:

* Biofuels take up a huge amount of land.
* Some of the trees planted have harmful effects on the atmosphere.
* The land used for biofuels should instead be used to grow crops to help feed the hungry.

For practice (page 15)

Match up each of the short summaries in the table with the number of the paragraph in the article to which it relates.

Paragraph	Main point
1	Anecdote about the writer's daughter sitting an entrance exam.
2	Girls today face many different kinds of pressure.
3	Young women today are likely to be more dissatisfied with their lives than those of the previous generation.
4	There are many examples of high-achieving women acting as role models for girls.
5	High-achievers expect everyone to share similar ambitions.
6	Successful people think that women who choose a domestic role lack ambition.
7	Women who work in lower-skilled jobs or who stay at home may find their lifestyle satisfying.
8	Not all young women aspire to reaching the top of the business world.
9	Women should be free to choose the role in life that suits them best.

II ANALYSING THE STYLE
SENTENCE STRUCTURE

For practice (page 20)

Comment on the types of sentences used in the pieces of writing. If the paragraphing is noteworthy in any way, say briefly what is special about it. Then discuss what effects the writers are aiming at.

1. *New Jaguar:*

   Rhetorical questions are used to create a conversational tone, as if the writer is anticipating questions the reader may ask about the car.

   Similarly, short sentences beginning with exclamations like 'Well' and 'Ah' create a sense that the writer is speaking directly to the reader.

   Balanced structures are used at times, either to create contrast ('admiration'/'mirth') or to suggest the car exhibits all-round qualities ('supreme looks'/'refined mechanics').

2. *Dead Souls:*

   Second sentence beginning 'Or' and fourth sentence beginning 'But' could have been joined to the previous ones. They are separated in order to heighten the contrast between the statements. Short sentence 'But this raised unanswerable questions' is followed by a series of rhetorical questions, which convey a sense of how little is known.

   The sentence structure throughout the paragraph creates a jumpy, staccato effect to mirror the progression of the writer's thoughts, and the fact that, in the absence of facts, he is speculating on what may have happened.

3. *Tudor Cottage Furniture sale:*

   In this advertisement, commands predominate. The many imperative verbs and verb phrases: 'want it, have it… enjoy… pay nothing… come… treat yourself… take advantage… amaze… click… visit… call… ', seize the reader's attention and try to manipulate the reader into doing what the advertisement wants. The paragraphs are short to make it very easy to assimilate all the elements of the advert: what it is selling, for how much, and where and how to buy it.

4. *'Uneasy Homecoming':*

   Sentence structure throughout this paragraph aims to build up an increasing sense of tension and unease.

   Long fourth sentence contrasts with the abrupt 'It was' to stress how Connie's insecurity led her to make an unnecessary check on the window.

   The ellipsis after 'If the lights had been seen across the bay…' allows her thoughts to trail off and leaves the reader to imagine what the consequences might be if the lights had been seen.

   The series of very short sentences, some of them minor sentences, towards the end builds up a crescendo of fear, as the reader waits to find out what happens.

   The single sentence paragraph at the end brings the tension to a climax.

5. *Glasgow for Free*:
   Many sentences are in the form of commands: 'do pay a visit…' The writer is trying to persuade the reader to follow his advice. The use of the future tense in 'You'll be fascinated…' continues in this persuasive style. The use of the second person, 'you', is colloquial as it sets up a conversational tone with the reader. There are also statements that give information. The last line of the entry is in note form. The bold type in 'Open' draws attention to this being an important piece of information for the reader. It is followed by a colon, which introduces the exact times and days.

6. *Bridget Jones's Diary*:
   Sentences are short and many are in note form. The layout with days and times shows this to be an extract from a diary. It is written in a typically abbreviated diary style, omitting some personal pronouns, verbs and articles: 'Was just leaving…'; 'Unexpected surprise'; 'card is still here.' The use of colloquialisms like 'Humph' adds to the informality of the style.

7. *Parliamentary report*:
   The writer begins with a statement that sets the scene: members of parliament are waiting for the Prime Minister to appear. The writer then uses a series of very short sentences, which act like a commentary to build tension around the Prime Minister's non-appearance.
   In the first paragraph he intersperses very short statements with even shorter minor sentences ('Then ten … Oh dear.'), ending with a question to reflect the thoughts of the people waiting. This tension-building technique is intensified in the second paragraph as he explores the surreal image of the PM being strangled by red tape. The sentences get shorter and shorter, all minor sentences, and one even has just one word: 'Remorseless.'
   The third paragraph begins with a statement that contrasts by being longer in length and thus breaks the tension. The two short final statements seem to reflect the sighs of relief.

For practice (page 24)

Discuss the purpose of the punctuation marks in the extracts.

1. Use of colon to introduce a list.
2. Use of semicolon to show link between two halves of sentence, the second half being a consequence of the first.
3. Semicolon creates a contrast between the two halves of the second sentence.
4. In the first sentence the colon introduces a list of colours. In the second sentence, semicolons are used to split up the items in the list.
5. Use of a dash to introduce a parenthesis that adds an extra piece of information or an explanation.
6. Semicolon used to create contrast between the two parts of the sentence.
7. Words contained between the two dashes are examples of the things that 'interested me'. An example of parenthesis.
8. Semicolons split up the description into its different aspects: mountains, trees, fields, etc.
9. Parentheses enclosed by dashes enable the author to insert her own feelings and reactions in the midst of the description; repeated use of these creates a sense of rapid thought and excitement.
10. Colon introduces a list of alternative explanations, each of which is separated from the one that follows by a semicolon. Dash used before adding on an extra piece of information.

For practice (page 25)

The writer uses an example of parenthesis (marked by a pair of dashes) in each paragraph. Can you identify what her purpose is in each example?

- Paragraph 1: 'almost half!' is humorously emphatic, drawing the reader's attention to the statistics. The exclamation mark adds a tone of amazement at the size of the figure spent in restaurants, showing the writer's own opinion.
- Paragraph 2: 'fittingly' adds a comment, giving her opinion that it was appropriate that the mass market restaurants began the trend for eating out among the wider population.
- Paragraph 3: 'namely fun' adds some extra information, identifying the feature that was lacking in fancier restaurants.

For practice (page 28)

Comment on the effectiveness of any feature of sentence structure in reinforcing the writer's opinion.
(2 marks)

	Answer	Mark awarded	Strengths/weaknesses
1	The sentence structure is effective as the writer uses parenthesis and a minor sentence.	0	This answer identifies two sentence structure features but does not comment on how these are effective in reinforcing the writer's opinion.
2	This is effective as the writer uses parenthesis to include an extra comment to show how bad Darien was.	1	This answer identifies one sentence structure feature without using quotation as evidence and makes a rather weak comment on what this feature achieves. It just manages to scrape 1 mark.
3	The writer's use of sentence structure is effective as the minor sentence ('Except Scotland.') is used to create a strong contrast with the previous statement (that the rest of the world has forgotten Darien). This conveys the writer's opinion that the Scots had made a serious error in going there.	2	This is a good answer as it comments fully on how the chosen feature of sentence structure (a minor sentence) reinforces the writer's opinion.
4	The writer uses parenthesis to insert his own comment in the midst of the fourth sentence ('quite rightly'). This shows that he is endorsing the opinion that the rest of the world was correct to show little interest in this remote place.	2	This is a good answer as it comments fully on how the chosen feature of sentence structure (parenthesis) reinforces the writer's opinion.

For practice (page 29)

Explain how the writers of the extracts use sentence structure effectively.

1. Use of repetition (series of expressions on the pattern of a verb followed by the word 'any' followed by a noun). These are arranged in ascending order of importance, building up to a climax. Antithesis is also used ('support'/'oppose' and 'friend'/'foe').
2. Series of exclamations designed to show a feeling of relief and elation.
3. First sentence is a rhetorical question, which is a more effective way of putting over the point as no one would be likely to say that they would prefer to be slaves than free men. The sentence is also an example of antithesis, as it contains balanced opposites ('living' versus 'dead' and 'die all slaves' versus 'live all free men').

4. An example of antithesis. 'Worse' contrasts with 'better' and 'should not have been invited' contrasts with 'should not have come'. Structures are parallel/symmetrical in that both subordinate clauses begin with 'if' and both principal clauses begin with 'I'.

5. This extract aims to create suspense by keeping the identity of 'something different' until the short sentence at the end ('It was a girl.'). The last sentence is deliberately short to contrast with the longer one preceding it. This adds impact and humour.

6. The whole extract is basically an expansion of the short opening statement, 'Fog everywhere.' This is a minor sentence as it contains no verb, which gives added impact. The constant repetition of the word 'fog' emphasises how it worked its way into every aspect of the scene, from the large areas of landscape to the smallest craft on the river. The verb 'is' is omitted in all the principal clauses.

7. An example of climax. The build-up is assisted by the use of alliteration on the letter 'c'. The disagreements between mother and daughter escalate from criticisms to corrections and end up with violence: 'I even threw her own china at her'.

8. Another list building up to a climax: 'be free one day'. The length of the list also effectively conveys how long and difficult the struggle will be before this freedom is finally achieved.

9. Although the second sentence beginning with 'But' could have been joined to the first, it is separated in order to create a greater contrast between 'generous' and 'prudent'. The words 'he now had four children' are in parenthesis. A colon is used to introduce the 'two factors'. The last sentence contains an element of balance and could therefore be said to make use of antithesis.

10. The colon is used to introduce a list of all the different types of dancers. The list is arranged as a series of antitheses ('gracefully'/'awkwardly', etc.). The second sentence is split into short sections divided by semicolons. Each section describes a stage in the dance, thus conveying an idea of regular, rhythmical movements.

WORD CHOICE

For practice (page 34)

Can you translate the extract into modern standard English?

The farm buildings at Peesie's Knapp (Lapwing Hill) were not more than twenty years old, but rather poor quality nevertheless. The house faced the road, which was convenient as long as you didn't mind that you couldn't even change your shirt without some bad mannered fellow staring in at you.

For practice (page 37)

Pick out two or three examples each from the extract of:

a) *informal language or slang*

b) *dialect*

c) *jargon.*

Draw a table and enter your examples in the appropriate columns.

Informal language or slang	Dialect	Jargon
Good heavens!	Me good dog	Eczema
Don't you?	Aye	Mange
I'm afraid so	Ah think	Myxoedema
Of course I am	Husband o' mine	Hypothyroidism
Well…	He's a gawp	Bradycardia
Wait a minute	The great lubbert	Thyroid deficiency
Oh yes	Knows nowt	
	All t'time	

For practice (page 38)

Look again at the quotation from President John F. Kennedy.

With a partner, discuss Kennedy's word choice and work out where words are being used literally and where they are being used figuratively.

'Bear any burden' is used figuratively; 'pay any price' is also figurative, although it could be taken literally.

IMAGERY

For practice (page 41)

Comment on the effectiveness of the writers' use of imagery in the examples.

1. Comparison of the house to a dinosaur suggests various similarities: it is obsolete; it takes up a great deal of space; it consumes a great deal; and so on. The comparison to a fossil continues the idea of something prehistoric lingering on into the modern age. Both are examples of metaphors.

2. Onomatopoeia is used in the word 'putted' to imitate the soft sound made by the flickering of the gas jet. The simile 'like a sick man's heart' compares the action of the gas to the irregular flutter of the heart of a dying patient. Another simile, 'mysterious as a chapel', introduces the idea of a religious atmosphere, which is continued in other similes that follow ('tapers', 'icons', etc.). A number of the descriptive effects here are based on the contrast of light and dark.

3. This extract depends on an extended metaphor comparing the guitar instructor to a doctor. His guitar case is compared to a doctor's bag; he asks the 'patient' how he is feeling; he tests his coordinations and gives him exercises as if they were a prescription. The exercises will 'cure' the student's faulty playing just as a prescription will cure a patient's illness.

4. 'Skewer-like' is appropriate as a skewer is a long, thin utensil used for piercing meat. This makes the dagger seem lethal and horrific. 'Like a hen' suggests the frantic fluttering a hen makes when picked up or frightened, and reveals the victim's panic. It also shows him as a rather pathetic, defenceless figure, lacking in dignity or courage. 'Like so much sawdust' emphasises the inertness of the dead body. Sawdust would be shapeless and lifeless; it also has no value. It is associated with stuffed dolls, also suggesting lifelessness.

5. The comparison of the rain to glass splinters effectively conveys how sharp and penetrating the rain was and suggests it hit the people with such force that it was almost like a series of physical attacks. It also has connotations of pain: being wounded by glass splinters would be extremely painful.

6. Two images are combined for humorous effect: the unruly, aggressive behaviour of shoppers on the first day of a sale, and a St Trinian's lacrosse match. St Trinian's is a fictional girls' school famous for over-the-top violence. This comically exaggerates how aggressive and unruly the women MPs were in their heckling of the Prime Minister.

7. The image is a comic one of hens pecking at the ground. Just as hens seem to spend a lot of time apparently pecking at nothing on the bare earth, so the Opposition MPs seem to be putting in a lot of effort complaining about nothing.

8. The image is of an unkempt bearded man with pieces of food stuck in the hairs of his beard. This is a striking image as it suggests houses perched at strange, precarious angles among the vegetation as if they might collapse down the side of the hill at any moment.

9. A 'safe pair of hands' is a metaphor from cricket. It means a player who will not let down his team by dropping a catch. The Defence Secretary is therefore seen as reliable, though dull. This is the image he presents 'at the dispatch box', which is where ministers from the front bench stand to speak in Parliament. The image of his conversation is of a tall glass of champagne, a sparkling wine that makes people tipsy quickly, suggesting his conversation has this uplifting effect. (This seems to be suggested ironically, since he is so dull in public.)

10. The image is of a bee that has gone into a jam jar in search of sweet jam and cannot get out. Just as bees buzz frantically if they are trapped inside something and never stop trying to escape, *The Apprentice* candidate never stopped moving or talking.

11. 'Let off steam' is an image from steam engines. When the pressure inside grew too high, a valve had to be opened to release steam or the engine would explode. In the same way, the dogs have to release the energy pent up inside them or they will become difficult to handle. The fruit image of 'a few rotten apples' applies to a fruit crop where most of the fruit is fine but just one or two are not. In the same way, most dogs behave well in parks and do not deserve to be banned from running about.

12. Newcastle's new manager used various images connected with sailing a ship. Just as 'plugging the leak holes and battening down the hatches' stops a ship taking on water that might sink it and stop it sailing, so the manager hoped to solve the various problems of the club and make it successful. The writer mocks the rather excessive and pretentious use of imagery by continuing with more sea images. 'Kwells' are anti-seasickness pills and being 'queasy' is a symptom of seasickness, as if the manager's over-the-top language made the writer feel ill.

For practice (page 46)

- *Identify which literary techniques are used in the extracts.*
- *Consider why the writer has used that technique. What effect is he or she trying to achieve?*

1. This extract defines circumlocution: 'determined to use five words where one would do', and gives two examples. The writer also uses a parody of Julius Caesar's words in: 'came and saw and stunned'.

2. Alliteration of the letter 'm' – appropriate because it strengthens the idea of a dark, monotonous scene. There is also an example of antithesis after the colon.

3. Pun on 'ties':
   articles of clothing that are bound round the neck, often used as Christmas gifts for men
   girls who are unattached and looking for a permanent relationship, which they hope to achieve by buying a gift for someone.

4. A play on words – 'top of the chocs', an analogy with *Top of the Pops* – is used to describe the best Easter egg.

5. Hyperbole, used for humorous effect.

6. Member of Parliament speaks in emotive language (e.g. 'savage cuts'). The Government Minister replies in a formal style that tries to make the measures seem less severe (e.g. 'to see if economies can be made'). This is an example of euphemism or circumlocution.

7. 'Interment' is a euphemism for 'buried', while 'incineration' is a euphemism for 'cremated'.

8. Words such as 'thou', 'heartily do I wish', etc., identify this extract as an example of archaic language.

9. A parody of sports journalism, employing many clichés typical of the genre, such as 'a game of two halves', 'flirted with disaster', 'pull the trigger', and so on. The metaphors have been overused to the point that they have lost the impact of the original images.

10. The humour of this passage derives from the fact that the author identifies pretentious hyperbole being used in the menu's descriptions of the dishes available ('Cumbrian Air-dried Ham', etc.), and then imitates and extends this in increasingly exaggerated ways, e.g. 'horizontal walking surface anterior to my feet', which simply means the floor. The passage ends with an effective anti-climax, contrasting the previous inflated language with the down-to-earth simplicity of the 'Sweets Menu'.

TONE

For practice (page 51)

The Circumlocution Office (from *Little Dorrit* by Charles Dickens).

Choose three examples of irony that you think are particularly effective, and try to explain why you have chosen them.

Possible examples include:

- the tongue-in-cheek comment that the Office was 'the most important Department' when it clearly is not
- the parenthesis 'as everyone knows without being told', although in reality no one believes this
- the ridiculous idea that the Gunpowder Plot could not have been stopped until vast amounts of paperwork had been done first – even when the match was due to be lit in half an hour
- the hyperbole of the list of details ('half a bushel of minutes', etc.)
- ironic tone in many expressions, e.g. 'glorious establishment', 'bright revelation', 'shining influence', 'delicate perception', which convey precisely the opposite.

For practice (page 52)

Can you re-write the passage in a non-emotive way?

Footballers do not play anywhere else in the world in front of large crowds that are so bitter, hostile and biased. I have never experienced another place where a sporting contest is accompanied by a symbolic song commemorating a battle fought over 300 years ago.

For practice (page 52)

Can you pick out the ways in which the writer uses emotive language to engage the reader's interest?

Feature	Examples
hyperbole	'war on the rhino butchers'; 'the beleaguered animal'
words denoting powerful sensations and emotions	'magnificent'; 'appallingly'; 'a suppurating open wound'; 'harrowing'
many adjectives and adverbs	'heavily pregnant'; 'magnificent'; 'hideously'; 'swiftly'
a dramatic and emotional tone	'would become appallingly clear'; 'hacked from her skull'; 'rampaged off'; 'hideously disfigured'; 'riddled with bullets'; 'the genocide of the rhino'; reference to 'gold, heroin or cocaine.'
vivid imagery (simile and metaphor)	'William's war on the rhino butchers'; 'Death did not come quickly'; 'ripped into her hide'; 'mown down'
anecdotes likely to arouse emotion	Story of pregnant rhino dying slowly; delivery of dead 'almost perfectly formed baby'.
striking sentence structure patterns	Very short opening sentence is dramatic; third sentence uses inversion to throw emphasis on 'opened fire'; short last sentence ends dramatically with reference to gold and drugs.

For practice (page 54)

Match the tone of each extract with one of the descriptions of tone given.

a) light-hearted; informal; humorous; chatty; informative – passage 6
b) reflective; formal; intellectual; thoughtful – passage 5
c) emotive; angry; emotional; personal – passage 3
d) impersonal; formal; factual, discursive, balanced and impartial – passage 2
e) personal; humorous; conversational; informal; rueful – passage 4
f) rhetorical; impassioned; inspiring; positive – passage 1
g) ironic; sarcastic, mocking; scathing – passage 7

Give two or three pieces of evidence to justify your choices.

Passage 1. f) rhetorical; impassioned; inspiring; positive:

- Although this extract is from a speech to be delivered orally, it is formal in style. Abbreviations are avoided in favour of full words: 'cannot'.
- The language is elevated (grand): 'the accumulated treasures of the thoughts of mankind'.
- The rhetorical tone is obtained through frequent repetition: 'the content of… the content of…'; 'we cannot succeed without… we cannot succeed without…'
- There are also lists of phrases with rhythmic cadences appropriate for speaking aloud: 'in your libraries, in your laboratories, in your conversations,' etc.

Passage 2. d) impersonal; formal; factual, discursive, balanced and impartial:

- The discursive tone is shown by the careful structuring of the argument, marked by words like 'moreover' and 'finally'.
- Ideas are presented using impersonal constructions beginning with 'it': 'It always seems…'; 'it must be remembered…' Formal expressions such as 'deemed' are preferred.
- The word 'I' is not used, nor personal opinions given. Although the expression 'appallingly badly paid' sounds emotive, it is backed up by figures that show it is literally true.
- There are many facts, such as the list of furnishings to be found in the steward's room.

Passage 3. c) emotive; angry; emotional; personal:

- Personal details such as references to 'husband and children' and personal anecdotes like the child's encounter with the dog are included. Personal tone is maintained by frequent use of 'I', 'me', 'my', 'us', etc.
- Many words refer to the emotions of the writer: 'enjoying'; 'felt good'; 'dislike'; 'loathing.'
- Angry tone shown in hostile description of dog as 'unleashed', 'gate-crash', 'hairy beast' and 'thumping great pet'; and of the owner's attitude: 'breath-taking indifference'. Anger is also directly expressed in extreme terms, e.g. 'inflame my loathing'.
- The incident of the dog knocking over the child is described in exaggerated terms, milking the drama: 'my trembling daughter'; 'tried to soothe her tears'; 'traumatised child'.
- Emotive tone is achieved with the use of many words expressive of extremes: 'intolerable, sanctimonious'; and the use of hyperbole: 'dreadful strain of humanity is a breed apart'; 'countless occasions'.

Passage 4. e) personal; humorous; conversational; informal; rueful:

- Personal tone is set up with references to members of his family and his university, and anecdotes about these. There is frequent use of personal pronoun 'I'.
- Conversational tone is achieved by use of second person: 'You'd have thought'. This gives the impression of chatting with the reader. The use of abbreviations adds to the informal tone.

- Informal expressions like 'nippers' and 'pals' add to the conversational tone, although the writer also uses some formal words rather self-consciously, so that the effect is quite humorous: 'upon disembarking, my grown-up life commenced.'
- Humorous tone is established with the joke about his parents giving him luggage to get rid of him, and the huge amount of it although he wasn't going far. His parody of being in court, pleading guilty to being 'too nice' with dialogue: 'M'lud, I am guilty as charged.'
- Humorous tone becomes rueful when he describes how his sons have taken advantage of his being 'too nice', so that he has become a 'janitor-come-chambermaid'. His complaints are made fondly and are not serious, however.

Passage 5. b) reflective; formal; intellectual; thoughtful:
- Reflective tone is achieved through the subject matter, which is an exploration of abstractions, shown by use of many abstract nouns: 'society'; 'neighbourliness'; 'education'; 'class'; 'nostalgia'.
- Many words to do with thinking are used: 'feels'; 'a sense of'; 'imagine'.
- Although written in the first person, the use of the plural 'we' is reflective. It includes the reader, so the tone remains fairly formal and impersonal; there are no references to individual feelings and experiences.
- Diction is intellectual: 'gargantuan'; 'tribal ghettos'; and the expression very formal: 'people pursue contact with one another…'
- Thoughtful tone is achieved through addition of random ideas, such as that in the last sentence: 'Once we are past the age of thirty…'; or the comment that it is unusual to start a conversation with a stranger.

Passage 6. a) light-hearted; informal; humorous; chatty; informative:
- Light-hearted tone set up by joking about how painters' names rhyme, all having two syllables ending in 'et'. Refers to eminent artist Gustave Courbet as 'Gus'.
- Use of irony in reference to daring 'to paint such unworthy subjects as real people' is light-hearted in tone, but also informative.
- Informal tone is established with use of minor sentences from the start and throughout. Abbreviations, e.g. 'that's' and 'wasn't', are also typical of informal writing. Use of exclamation marks – 'Manet used black!!' – is typical of informal writing and here used to highlight that using this colour was surprising in some way.
- Slang is used frequently, e.g. 'these gents'.
- The use of parentheses containing chatty comments ('*Quel horreur!*'; 'deep breath') adds to the humorous, conversational tone. Colloquialisms like 'eh?' and questions 'Why and how?' give the impression of chatting to the reader.
- Passage is informative, however, providing facts about art, such as names of paintings ('Burial at Omans') and information on technique ('the opposition of light and shade'), albeit in a jokey tone.

Passage 7. g) ironic; sarcastic, mocking; scathing:
- Exclamation: 'how shameful…' seems to have a sympathetic, emotive tone until it is undercut by the ridiculous reasons for staff being called 'poor' and being 'forced to work', which then shows the tone to be ironic. It becomes clear that the writer is mocking the BBC staff for complaining that their environment wasn't 'creative' or 'inspiring' enough, and being sarcastic at their expense, since most people have more serious things to complain about.
- 'Thankfully' is also heavily ironic, as the writer clearly thinks the 'big budget makeover' is a waste of money on such a pretext. Calling the offices 'creative wastelands' is seen to be sarcastic, as it goes on to say that the offices being complained about are very new and cost a great deal. This tone is continued when he calls the BBC staff 'victims of creativity deprivation'. Such pretentious language may be seen as typical of the jargon they use themselves.

- Quoting the cost – '£1 billion building' – is scathing as this is a huge amount of money for something that is already being complained of as unsatisfactory. The tone becomes more seriously critical with the use of a colloquialism, 'dishing out', used of the substandard programmes being transmitted, and 'bucket-loads of cash' to highlight the waste of public money.
- 'Perhaps, while they're at it, they might dispense with…' has an ironic tone, as he knows this will not happen, but he uses it to introduce his complaints about the programming being poor, despite the amount of money being spent at the BBC.

III EVALUATION AND COMPARISON

Specimen plan (page 62)

(Answers to questions are on pages 52–56.)

Evaluate the effectiveness of the final paragraph as a conclusion to the passage as a whole. (**3 marks**)

Feature or idea made in conclusion	Links back to...
'Don't get me wrong' – humble, pleading tone, wanting readers to be on her side.	Contrasts effectively with earlier tone, which was confident, challenging and assertive. She said Chinese parents could 'get away with' things like forcing children to practise constantly or insulting them if they had less-than-perfect results. She herself had done this.
'It's not that Chinese parents don't care' – plea that the harsh regime has a loving basis.	Repeats her earlier assertion that when Chinese children do well the parents shower them with praise and boost their confidence.
Two short sentences, one a minor sentence, 'Just … children'.	Simplicity of sentence structure and wording creates tone of sincerity that emphasises that Chinese parents, like all parents, aim for the best for their children.
'just an entirely different parenting model' – conciliatory tone, acknowledges that the Chinese model is just one style, and that others may be valid.	This is likely to mollify the reader as it softens the apparently critical tone of her earlier comments, which seemed to suggest only the Chinese have got it right and Western parents are ineffective and too indulgent.

Specimen evaluation answer (page 62)

'Don't get me wrong' has a humble, pleading tone, as if Chua wants her readers to be on her side. This contrasts effectively with her earlier, more assertive tone when she was outlining examples of the strict discipline and study regimes that Chinese parents could 'get away with', and when she was being critical of the apparently feeble Western approach.

When she says, 'It's not that Chinese parents don't care', she makes a plea that the apparent harshness has a loving basis. This repeats her earlier assertion that 'plenty of ego-inflating parental praise' is 'lavished' on the children in private, and that Chinese parents devote long hours to helping them.

The two sentences 'Just … children' are both short and simple, the first a minor sentence, worded simply. This simplicity creates a tone of sincerity that emphasises her point that the 'tiger mother' just does what she thinks is best for her children.

When she says the Chinese employ 'just an entirely different parenting model', she seems to acknowledge that there are different approaches to parenting that may each be right. This softens the harshness of her earlier message, which seemed to imply that Western parents' methods were ineffective and only the Chinese methods were right. This ends the passage on a suitably conciliatory note likely to appeal to the reader.

(A bullet-pointed answer is shown on page 55.)

Specimen comparison answer (page 64)

Both passages look at the topic of bringing up children. Identify key areas where Jemima Lewis agrees or disagrees with Amy Chua.

You may answer this question in continuous prose or in a series of developed bullet points. (**5 marks**)

At first it appears that Jemima Lewis's attitude to being a parent is very different from Amy Chua's. While Chua endorses the Chinese practice of forcing children to work extremely hard and overcoming their reluctance, Lewis admits she is quite relaxed about how she brings up her children. While Chua sees academic excellence as paramount, and does not allow her children to be distracted from their school work, Lewis lets her children watch television and doesn't bother too much about their behaviour. Chua sees no problem in children being driven hard with 'practice, practice, practice', while Lewis obviously sees making children practise piano scales 'till their fingers throb' as wrong. Her negative tone in 'barking out instructions' shows she would not behave in such a way herself.

However, Lewis does not join in the general criticism of the 'tiger parent'. She admits she herself is often 'too tired and busy' to take her children to activities, showing she believes she could make more of an effort. Lewis disagrees with the 'boo/hiss' attitude of the critics who turn well-meaning parents like Chua into 'bogeymen', and obviously thinks it wrong to compare them to neglectful and abusive parents who don't make any effort at all. She clearly disagrees with demonising the 'tiger mother' as a 'gimlet-eyed Lady Macbeth'. Just as Chua says that pushing children hard shows how much parents care, Lewis accepts that while the over-enthusiastic father may embarrass his children he is making an effort to help them. She agrees with Chua that the behaviour of such parents, although some may see it as over the top, is 'evidence of love'.

(The full list of bullet points is shown on page 56.)

Note

- Each paragraph begins with a 'topic sentence'. The first introduces the differences, while the second topic sentence acts as a link to introduce the similarities in their views.

- Comparisons and contrasts are interwoven, giving equal space to both writers. This is preferable to listing all the points of one writer, followed by all the points from the other.

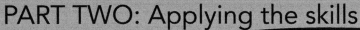

FOCUS ON READING 1

Football Results (pages 68–70)

a) As a result of modern technology, information can now be accessed instantly anywhere in the world, so that it is virtually impossible not to find out sports results (**2 marks**).

b) In line 1, the **ellipsis** indicates that the statement could be continued. He begins with a clichéd expression used at the end of weekend news bulletins when the sports announcer tells viewers: 'If you don't want to know the score, then look away now.' The reader expects the statement to be finished in the usual way but instead the writer uses the ellipsis to introduce his own original comment: '…well, pack up your things and move to an uninhabited island somewhere in the South Pacific.' This adds an element of surprise and humour.

Sentence lengths: first sentence is reasonably long; the second is very short; the third is long. This makes the short sentence in the middle ('It's your only hope.') stand out more.

The third sentence begins with a **conjunction**, 'And'. Normally, this would not be recommended; the second and third sentences could be joined together with 'and', but this would be less effective. After the short, definite statement 'It's your only hope', there follows a list of other ways in which it would still be impossible to avoid hearing the scores. Each item on the list is increasingly unlikely and far-fetched, reinforcing the writer's main point: that in the modern world it is impossible to be completely isolated from sources of information. (**1 mark for a brief comment; 2 marks for a more developed answer. Marks can be awarded as 2+2, 2+1+1 or 1+1+1+1.**)

c) The remainder of the paragraph expands on the statement that 'knowledge these days is instant' (**1 mark**) by using lists – e.g. all the various types of media used to convey information (**1 mark**).

d) 'It wasn't always so' points back to the current situation discussed in the previous section (i.e. the ease of accessing results) (**1 mark**) and contrasts this with the way things were in the past, which is developed in the paragraph to follow (**1 mark**).

e) The writer expands the point by giving examples of the difficulties (e.g. some clubs used scoreboards that were difficult to decipher; people would congregate outside shops selling TV sets to watch the results; some fans would have to wait until the results appeared in the next day's newspaper) (**1 mark for each**).

f) Expressions such as 'instantly dropped whatever they were doing', 'stuck wondering until the next morning' or 'dash out frantically' reveal that learning the results was so important that people would make this a matter of priority above other activities and would constantly be thinking about the subject until they could find out the information. Good answers will comment on the connotations of words such as 'instantly dropped', 'frantically', etc. (**1 mark for a valid point; 2 marks for a more developed answer.**)

g) At that time it was even more difficult to find out the results if you lived abroad because communications were more difficult (**2 marks**).

h) Possible answers (**for 3 marks each**) include:
   - Use of parenthesis in 'a full 40 hours after full-time' (**1 mark**) provides a commentary on the rest of the sentence (**1 mark**) by stressing the suspense involved in waiting to learn the results (**1 mark**).
   - Word choice of 'expedition' shows that he was prepared to make a journey into town to track down an English-language newspaper (**1 mark**). 'Expedition' has connotations of a complex excursion (**1 mark**) involving planning and preparation (**1 mark**).

i) **Advantage:** paraphrase of 'every bit of information available to them at the touch of a button' (e.g. any necessary data can be accessed quickly and easily) **(1 mark)**.

Disadvantage: paraphrase of 'inherent inability to hold conversations with other human beings without the use of an electronic device' (e.g. people are now so involved in using technology to communicate that they do not talk to each other personally) **(1 mark)**.

j) 'Instant gratification' has negative connotations: people are impatient and not prepared to wait **(1 mark)**.

Tone of '24 hours solid' is also negative, suggesting that availability of information is excessive **(1 mark)**.

Reference to 1960s' TV programme suggests he shares the outlook of football fans of that era **(1 mark)**.

Extra question (page 70)

In your own words, summarise the main point from each paragraph, omitting evidence and examples.

1. There is literally nowhere a person can go to avoid finding out football results.
2. The variety of media available today ensures that results can be learnt instantly anywhere in the world.
3. In the past it was not so easy to find out the results.
4. Even spectators who were present at a match found it difficult to follow the score.
5. On Saturday nights some people would position themselves outside shops selling television sets in order to watch the results.
6. Those who could not find out the results in this way or by asking other people would have to wait until the next day's newspapers appeared.
7. Discovering the results was even more difficult for those who lived abroad.
8. A special journey into the city centre to find an English-language newspaper would be necessary.
9. Rather than buying a copy, as a student the author would try to flick through the paper to find the results and then put it back on the shelf.
10. Such experiences are hard for younger people to understand as they are so familiar with modern means of communication.
11. The young can access information at any time in a way that was impossible in the 1960s.

FOCUS ON READING 2

The Crombie Coat (pages 71–73)

a) 'wonderful wardrobe'; 'sacred sonic screwdriver'; 'neo-Victorian velvet'; 'Brideshead nostalgia boom'. (**1 mark for each of up to three examples.**)

b) 'sacred' usually means something respected for being holy (**1 mark**); *Doctor Who* is just TV light entertainment, although some viewers take it very seriously. The writer is gently mocking devotees of the programme (**1 mark**).

c) **Informal:** 'can't'; 'twinge of envy'; 'an interesting bunch'; 'and so on'.
Formal: 'opportunities extended to…'; 'latest incarnation'; 'dandyism of early seventies Britain'.
(**2 marks for at least one example each of formal/informal.**)

d) 'clobber' (**1 mark**)

e) Just as a 'palimpsest' is a manuscript on which traces of earlier messages can be read (**1 mark**), so the Crombie coat reminds us of the history of succeeding generations who have used the coat in different contexts (**1 mark**).

f) • It attracted attention at the Great Exhibition of 1851.
   • It was a major item of British export, being sent as far afield as America, France and Russia.
   • People went to great pains to acquire it, such as crossing a blockade or using a hot-air balloon to get it.

   (**1 mark for each.**)

g) The anecdote illustrates that the coat was very hard wearing, having lasted so long. It must have still been in good condition for the owner to have suggested putting a new lining in such an old coat. It also illustrates that people get so attached to their Crombie coats they will do anything to keep them wearable. (**Any two for 1 mark each.**)

h) 'The ruling elite of the Soviet Union' (**1 mark**).

i) 'tribal subcultures': the image is of a primitive ethnic group. Such groups have characteristic clothes and marks of identity; in the same way adolescent gangs dress and behave in a distinctive way. It suggests the rather wild nature of these gangs.
'a sort of magic that knows no barrier': a magic word or object can enable people to do supernatural things like pass through locked doors or achieve amazing feats; in the same way, the Crombie coat allows the wearer to do things they would not be able to without it.
'hovers over': the image is of an angel (or bird), suggesting something that due to its elevation is superior and of dominating importance (compared with other garments).
'laureate of late twentieth-century urban style': a laureate (literally meaning crowned with laurel) is someone who is regarded as the best in their field; this suggests Elms is the recognised leader of fashion of his time.
'moment of epiphany': an epiphany is a sense of profound enlightenment, usually used of a religious experience. In the same way, putting on this iconic coat was particularly special.
(**Any one example clearly explained for 2 marks, or two examples more briefly explained.**)

j) Early skinheads were mainly concerned with style and fashion and were successors to the fashionable 'mods' of the '60s (**1 mark**); later skinheads were known as violent savages with right-wing tendencies (**1 mark**).

k) **Sentence structure:** the third sentence begins with a series of phrases/clauses before the main clause 'I saw…' and leads up to the final inversion (within the noun clause) of 'there in the window was the coat.' The next sentence is a list of descriptive, adjective phrases. This is followed by two dramatic short sentences leading to the climax of 'the dream'.

Word choice: dramatic phrases such as: 'waited almost a quarter of a century'; 'after 24 long years'; 'a dream was about to be realised'. The phrase, 'a certain Crombie and Sons of Aberdeen, Scotland' has a portentous tone, suggesting something amazing is promised.
Word order: the inversion in the phrase: 'there in the window was the coat' creates drama by putting 'the coat' in the position of most emphasis at the very end of a long sentence. (**At least two features for 4 marks. Marks can be awarded as 2+2, 3+1 or 1+1+1+1, depending on quality of comment.**)

l) • He had wanted to have a coat like this since he was a child (**1 mark**).
    • He had waited a lifetime to become the possessor of such a coat (**1 mark**).
    • The name 'Crombie' on the label was a guarantee that it was the real thing: it was the iconic coat (**1 mark**).
    • It is a very warm, practical garment that is enjoyable to wear (**1 mark**).
    (**Any three for 3 marks.**)

m) He lists very important and dramatic situations in which the coat was used: by British soldiers fighting for their country in the First World War and as the public uniform of the top officials in the Soviet Union, one of the most powerful and aggressive countries in the world (**2 mark**). He ends on a humorous note by referring to the 'Daleks and Cybermen', which are not real, just the science-fiction characters against which Doctor Who has to battle in the TV programme, thus achieving an anti-climax (**2 mark**).
    (**Any combination which includes ideas from each paragraph for maximum of 3 marks.**)

Extra questions (page 73)

1. *What do you think is the main purpose of this article? Is it to inform, to entertain, or to reflect? Explain your reasons.*
   A case can be made for all three purposes:
   • **Information:** different styles of costume worn by various incarnations of Doctor Who; history of Crombie coats given in paragraph 2; widening fame and success of coat described in paragraphs 3–5.
   • **Entertainment:** amusing expression used to describe *Doctor Who* costumes in paragraph 1; colloquial expressions such as 'clobber'; amusing anecdote (about relining an ancient Crombie) in paragraph 4; account of Robert Elms's acquisition of a Crombie and his feelings for it; the use of hyperbole in describing buying the coat as 'a moment of epiphany'.
   • **Reflection:** writer reflects on the 'wardrobe opportunities' offered by the programme in paragraph 1; paragraph 2 has a reflective tone, 'as a metaphor for the state of the nation…', etc. He also reflects on the democratic appeal of Crombie coats in paragraphs 6 and 7.

   (**Up to 4 marks may be given for an answer suggesting one or more of these purposes with appropriate back-up.**)

2. *Evaluate the effectiveness of the final paragraph as a conclusion to the whole passage.*
   The final paragraph sums up two of the most striking uses of Crombie coats in history (as uniforms in the First World War and standard wear of top Soviet Russian officials), which he had described in detail in paragraphs 4 and 5.
   He also reiterates the coat's use as the preferred gear of football fans, which reminds us of Robert Elms's enjoyment of his coat mentioned in paragraph 9.
   The final comment that it is 'more than equal to Daleks and Cybermen' is humorous since these are fictional, fantasy characters from *Doctor Who*. The humour arises from juxtaposing them with serious, real-life wearers of the coat. It ends the article on a topical note as he has written the article concerning a new development in the programme as Peter Capaldi takes over the lead role, having chosen a Crombie as his costume.
   (**Up to 5 marks may be given, depending on detail and quality of ideas. Answer may be in bullet points.**)

FOCUS ON READING 3

Scotland in Hollywood (pages 74–77)

a) **Sound:** 'Scawtchman' is humorous as it attempts to imitate Doohan's drawling Canadian accent.
Dialogue: the ridiculous, over-the-top use of dialect ('Ah cannae', etc.) is comic, as is the repetition of letters in 'haggisss' and 'sirrrrr' to represent an exaggerated attempt at speaking Scots. The words 'haggis' and 'noo' are typical caricatures of Scots speech.
Word choice: 'roared' is comical, as it suggests how energetically he delivered his lines, while his accent was really bad; 'Steely Caledonian stare' is a comical idea as Doohan is acting like the caricature of a tough Scotsman.
Irony: it is ironic that it is a Canadian who is insisting on playing the role as a Scot, when his accent is clearly so bad.
(Any combination of two or more for 4 marks.)

b) The US moguls thought it sounded down-to-earth, realistic and sincere, and believed it would appeal to American audiences who would not know it was not authentic **(1 mark)**.
The Scots found it totally unconvincing, unbelievable and cringeworthy **(1 mark)**.

c) 'Scotty' is the character in *Star Trek* played by James Doohan, whose bad playing of a Scotsman has just been discussed **(1 mark)**; '(probably not) the worst offender' leads on to some other examples of dreadful acting and bad Scottish accents **(1 mark)**.

d) The ellipsis makes us wait **(1 mark)**, and the surprise when we learn that Connery was cast as a Spaniard enhances the humour **(1 mark)**; as a Scot he was one of the few actors who could do an authentic Scottish accent, but he was having to pretend to be foreign **(1 mark)**. **(First point and one other for 2 marks.)**

e) 'Ancient, whimsical and charming' are all very vague adjectives, so we can guess how inauthentic the performances were **(1 mark)**.
'Lilting nonsense' is effective as 'lilting' suggests singing, which is not how real people speak **(1 mark)**, and 'nonsense' shows it cannot be understood, as does 'indecipherable' **(1 mark)**.
'Growl' is comically onomatopoeic, suggesting a primitive animal rather than a person, and is thus the opposite extreme to 'lilting' **(1 mark)**. **(Any two for 2 marks.)**

f) It was ironic that the film-makers chose to make a fake set in Hollywood, rather than use a genuine location in Scotland **(1 mark)**. Calling Scotland 'not Scottish enough' is ironic since obviously that is what Scotland actually is like, not some idealised concept held by the film-makers **(1 mark)**.

g) 'abomination' has religious connotations of something monstrous and offensive to God **(1 mark)**. The hyperbole is effective in expressing Norton's outrage that the real accents of the Scottish actors in *Gregory's Girl* should be suppressed in favour of fake dubbed ones **(1 mark)**.

h) This is an example of antithesis, a balanced contrast between the two parts of the sentence **(1 mark)**, where the subject in the first part – 'a Scotsman' – becomes the object in the second part – 'Scotsmen'; 'television' is the object in the first clause and then becomes the subject in the second one, with 'invented' being used in both clauses but in a punning way with different meanings, the first use being literal and the second metaphorical **(1 mark)**. **(1 mark for the first point, supported by appropriate explanation for 1 further mark.)**

i) (i)   Redmond means the kitschy Scottish images traditionally found on shortbread tins, such as tartan, heather, Scottie dogs, etc (**1 mark**).

  (ii)   'Tinnery' is a coinage (invented word). She has made an abstract noun from a common noun 'tin', to mean the use of these images (**1 mark**).

j)   Following the 'ancient land of…' comes a list of typically Scottish things. The first two items are quite serious associations of Scotland: 'castle, bagpipes' (**1 mark**), but where we might expect something grander like 'mountains', it ends with a comical idea: 'wee dugs like Greyfriars Bobby' (**1 mark**). The use of dialect in 'wee dugs' emphasises the humorous anti-climax (**1 mark**). **(First point and one other for 2 marks.)**

k)   Americans have a negative view of an English accent, and choose it for evil characters (**1 mark**); Scots accents are used positively and are seen as comical and sincere. They are also associated with the downtrodden and hence sympathised with (**1 mark**).

l)   Norton is a Scot, and as Gibson's accent sounded authentic to him, it cannot have been all that bad (**1 mark**). This view was shared by Scottish actors who worked with him, including James Cosmo (**1 mark**). It is also true that since Wallace lived so long ago he would speak in an archaic way that no one truly knows the sound of (**1 mark**). It also seems petty to criticise Gibson's accent since without him there would have been no film (**1 mark**).

m)   *Mickey Mouse* is a famous film cartoon that everyone finds funny. When the term is applied to something serious it implies a dumbing down. 'Mickey Mouse Scotland' would be a stupid, oversimplified portrayal without any basis in reality (**1 mark**).

n)   For *Brave*, Disney paid a lot of heed to getting the Scottish accents right (**1 mark**). Previously this was not done as it was thought American and foreign audiences would not understand Scots (**1 mark**). The producers of *Brave* believed the audiences would gradually acquire an ear for the accent as they viewed it (**1 mark**). Since the film was successful it is likely this approach will be followed in future (**1 mark**). **(Any two points for 2 marks.)**

Extra questions (page 77)

a)   Identify the writer's view of Scots accents in most Hollywood films.
Scots accents in Hollywood films are very poor, ridiculous and/or like a caricature; Scots are horrified by attempts to portray them (**1 mark**).

b)   *Explain any one play on words in the article's title and subtitle.*
'Shrek' is a pun on 'shriek'; this is appropriate as *Shrek* is one of the American films that makes use of the sort of Scottish accents that appal Scots audiences (**2 marks**).
'Lost for words' is also a play on words as it means shocked, but is also appropriate since it is the pronunciation of Scots words that is shocking (**2 marks**).
(Any one for maximum of 2 marks.)

FOCUS ON READING 4

Apprenticeships (pages 78–79)

a) Two points for 1 mark each. Possibilities include:
   - Rhetorical question raises a query that is answered in the next sentence.
   - First sentence contains a list of deliberately provocative descriptions of the young.
   - This provides a contrast to the next part of the argument, which argues that in fact the young are perfectly suited to the job of spying in the modern era.

b) 'tech-savvy': well-informed about all the latest developments in (computer) technology (**1 mark**). 'an apolitical outlook': do not have any strong loyalties to a political party (**1 mark**). 'a complete indifference to the concept of privacy': the young do not believe in keeping themselves to themselves; they are curious to know what others are doing (**1 mark**).

c) Students should be able to identify examples of technical jargon such as 'cyber-espionage', 'hacking', 'cybersecurity', etc (**1 mark**).
   Terms such as 'institutionalised', 'Data Center', 'training programme', etc, show how this new approach to spying is well-established, official, of central importance, etc (**1 mark**).

d) Ironic tone created by the contrast between a very small figure ('dozens') and a large statistic ('964,900') (**1 mark**). Contrast also between the excessively precise nature of this figure and the vagueness of 'dozens' highlights how the provision of these places will have no significant impact on the unemployment figures (**1 mark**).

e) There is currently too rigid a distinction between jobs suitable for graduates and non-graduates (**1 mark**). We should examine whether a university degree is really necessary for certain professions (**1 mark**).

f) Paraphrase of 'café assignations with mysterious Russians' and 'more sifting through mountains of ill-gotten computer data' e.g. arranging to meet in secret (**1 mark**) with agents from the opposite side (**1 mark**); searching through vast amounts of information (**1 mark**) gained by hacking into computers (**1 mark**).

g) 'Espionage is not the only profession that has changed' links back to the earlier discussion of how spying has become more hi-tech (**1 mark**).
   'not the only profession that should welcome an update to recruitment and training' links forward to the point developed in the rest of the passage, which is that the idea of apprenticeships should be developed further (**1 mark**).

h) 'capital' (**1 mark**) and 'accrue' (**1 mark**). Connotations of these words could be discussed in class – university as an investment for the future; involves a process of gradual acquisition of the necessary social skills, etc.

i) Image is one of glamour (excitement/danger/adventure, etc.) (**1 mark**).
   Reality involves 'tedium and petty stationery-based conflict' (boredom, routine tasks, correspondence over minor matters involving disagreement) (**1 mark**).

j) It would be necessary to convince potential students and their parents that the apprenticeship route would provide as many career advantages as the traditional route of university education (**2 marks**).

k) It reinforces the idea that people should follow the kind of job they are most suited to, rather than going for a choice of career that would be expected of them because of their background (**1 mark**). They should train for jobs for which there is a clear demand, rather than study academic subjects that may not enable them to find employment (**1 mark**).

Extra questions (page 79)

1. *In the first four paragraphs, the writer explores the idea of apprentice spies. How does the tone of this section contrast with her tone in the second half of the article? Use examples to illustrate your answer.*

    Contrast between subjective and objective approaches: earlier paragraphs give an opinion; later ones are more factual.

    First four paragraphs are more informal (e.g. conversational tone of 'That's what'; word choice of 'tech-savvy', etc.).

    Tone is cynical and mocking (e.g. use of '964,900'; references to 'wannabe agents', 'loiter', 'café assignations', etc.). Writer's opinion is made clear in the first four paragraphs.

    In the remaining paragraphs the article takes a more speculative approach, considering the issues involved in redesigning training programmes.

    Approach is more balanced, pointing out both advantages and difficulties.

    (Up to 4 marks, which can be awarded as 2+2, 2+1+1 or 1+1+1+1.)

2. *Using your own words as far as possible, sum up in bullet point form the arguments made by the writer in favour of apprenticeships. You should make at least four bullet points.*

    Any four of the following for 1 mark each:

    *   On-the-job training (learning while doing the job).

    *   A mapped-out career path (a clear progression to different levels throughout the person's working life).

    *   Other benefits we associate with a university degree, such as the provision of social capital (learning the skills of interacting with different kinds of people).

    *   May promote social equality (help those from less privileged backgrounds; change the attitude of middle-class people to trades).

    *   Increase individual job satisfaction (help people enjoy their work).

    *   Improve professional standards (create a higher quality of service).

PRACTICE PAPER 1

A Healthy Diet (pages 82–84)

Question	Expected response	Maximum mark	Additional guidance
1. a)	Candidates should explain two causes of anxiety. Candidates must use their own words. No marks are awarded for verbatim quotations from the passage. *Possible answers shown in the 'Additional Guidance' column.*	2	**Causes of anxiety (for 1 mark each):** • Alarmist headlines in newspapers suggest bacon is very dangerous. • Danger of eating bacon is comparable to smoking, widely known to be harmful to health and cause cancer. • Eating foods like bacon and cheese is said to cause cancer.
1. b)	Candidates should refer to at least two features of language, and analyse how the writer uses them to convey his meaning effectively. Marks will depend on the quality of comment. 2 marks may be awarded for a reference to a language feature plus detailed/insightful comment; 1 mark for reference plus more basic comment; 0 marks for reference alone. Marks can be awarded as 2+2, 2+1+1 or 1+1+1+1. *Possible answers shown in the 'Additional Guidance' column.*	4	**Sentence structure:** • Use of second person 'you'd'/'you've' draws in the reader who may have been eating bacon, a common food. **Word choice:** • 'you'd be forgiven…' suggests it is reasonable to be afraid. **Imagery:** • 'time-bomb ticking in your stomach': image of a bomb about to explode inside the body stresses life-threatening nature of the problem. **Tone:** • Tone of black humour in idea of threat from common foods like bacon sandwiches and carbonara conveys idea in satirical way.
2.	Candidates should identify **two or more** examples of imagery and explain how they are effective in illustrating the alarmist nature of reports on diet. Marks can be awarded as 2+2, 2+1+1 or 1+1+1+1. *Possible answers shown in the 'Additional Guidance' column.*	4	• 'bombarded': image of bombs being dropped suggests relentless barrage of scare stories. • 'addictive potential': image of drug addiction is worrying as it is life threatening – suggests meat may be equally dangerous. • 'headlines screamed': use of personification effective to suggest the large black newspaper headlines that seem to shout out their message in a threatening way. • 'what's-curing-me-and-killing-me-today merry-go-round': image of a fairground roundabout that goes round and round in a way that makes you dizzy. This illustrates how advice constantly changes, causing anxiety and confusion.

Question	Expected response	Maximum mark	Additional guidance
3.	Candidates should identify linking function in argument and the use of a question to introduce the next stage in it. 1 mark will be awarded for quoting a reference to the topic previously discussed and summarising it briefly; 1 mark will be awarded for quoting a reference to the new topic being introduced and summarising it briefly. 1 mark will be awarded for noting that a question is used to raise the next topic for discussion. *Possible answers shown in the 'Additional Guidance' column.*	3	• The author introduces the next stage in the argument by asking a question to which the answer will follow. • The question, 'Can eating burgers really be as bad for you as smoking?' refers back to the danger of eating meat that has been explored. • 'how we know how bad smoking is…' introduces the topic of the dangers of smoking and the evidence for them that will be the next topic.
4.	Candidates should identify two successful outcomes from research connecting health with lifestyle factors from lines 19–29. Candidates must use their own words. No marks are awarded for verbatim quotations from the passage. *Possible answers shown in the 'Additional Guidance' column.*	2	• Richard Doll discovered a common link between lung cancer and smoking when he studied a large group of men with the disease, and discovered virtually all were smokers. • Dr John Snow discovered that cholera was caused by contamination in the water supply
5. a)	Candidates should identify **four** reasons to account for the difficulty of pinpointing the effects of diet on health. Candidates must use their own words. No marks are awarded for verbatim quotations from the passage. *Possible answers shown in the 'Additional Guidance' column.*	4	• There are very few toxic substances that some people take in a lot of and others do not ingest at all. • It is difficult to say exactly that one particular food is beneficial as it is unreasonable to get someone to eat it for a prolonged period and compare them with someone else who does not. • People are unreliable when it comes to saying what they actually eat. • It is difficult to say eating a particular food makes someone healthy as other factors may be involved. • The body's metabolism is so complicated that it is easy to be wrong about what is and isn't healthy to eat. • There are many claims made for so-called healthy foods that are impossible to prove. • Although studies suggest certain foods are either bad or good for health, there is conflicting evidence for how far this is true, and experts disagree.

Question	Expected response	Maximum mark	Additional guidance
5. b)	Candidates should analyse how the writer's language conveys the meaning effectively. At least two examples should be given. Marks will depend on the quality of comment. There will be some overlap between different language features identified – this should not affect the mark. 2 marks may be awarded for a reference to a language feature plus detailed/insightful comment; 1 mark for reference plus more basic comment; 0 marks for reference alone. Marks can be awarded as 2+2, 2+1+1 or 1+1+1+1. *Possible answers shown in the 'Additional Guidance' column.*	4	**Sentence structure:** • Short sentence 'But smoking…' is blunt comment that most research is not so simple. • This short sentence acts as a link introducing problems of research, indicated by word 'but'. • Use of rhetorical question in lines 36–37 emphasises difficulty of interpreting research. • 'how can we know … live healthier lives generally' – use of antithesis emphasises idea of confusion. **Word choice:** • 'a course of celery' sounds ridiculous, highlighting the difficulty of conducting research. • 'pomegranate or chia seeds': references to strange and exotic foods illustrate eccentric theories on healthy diet. • 'plenty of fruit and veg': informal, simple language mimics the point that most results of research are fairly basic. **Imagery:** • 'smoking is a low-hanging fruit': such fruit is easier to pick than fruit growing higher up. In the same way, smoking was easier to blame for disease than other factors that were less easy to pin down. • 'tease out causes': image is of unravelling a tangled mass of thread/wool, illustrating difficulty of separating different factors that cause disease. • 'broader-brush factors': image is of painting roughly with large strokes, rather than fine detail. This illustrates the lack of precision in results from dietary research. **Contrast:** • 'Red meat [etc.] are all bad for you … fruit and veg is good for you' – shows some results are quite simplistic. • Contrast between simple language and formal technical language – 'epidemiologists', 'plausible hypotheses' – shows difficulty of relating scientific research to normal life. **Tone:** • Humorous, faux naïve tone set up through use of informal language – 'lots of humans … don't touch at all' – reveals difficulty of interpreting research. • Use of second person – 'you can't', 'You have to' – creates a conversational tone, as if pleading with the reader to understand the difficulties. • Mocking tone in reference to 'pomegranate or chia seeds … good for your liver, or whatever' – reveals contempt for self-styled diet 'experts' who don't know what they are talking about.

Question	Expected response	Maximum mark	Additional guidance
6.	Candidates should evaluate the final paragraph's effectiveness as a conclusion to the passage as a whole. Marks will depend on the quality of comment. For full marks there must be appropriate attention to the idea of a conclusion. A more basic comment may be awarded 1 mark. *Possible answers shown in the 'Additional Guidance' column.*	2	• Effective summing up of most research into effects of lifestyle on health as inconclusive: 'None of these studies is the final truth'. • Balanced deduction based on the evidence, which is not so alarmist as opening paragraph: 'probably a bit more dangerous than we previously thought' – this is reassuring to the reader. • Admission that some research is extremely valuable, like discovery of the cause of cholera, and scientists do advance our understanding of health. • Humorous tone of ending with very down-to-earth, non-scientific advice: 'what your mother told you: eat your greens and get plenty of exercise'. Makes impact through simplicity of style.
7.	Candidates should identify key differences and similarities in the two passages by referring in detail to both passages. There may be some overlap among the differences and similarities. Markers will have to judge the extent to which a candidate has covered two points or one. Candidates can use bullet points in this final question, or write a number of linked statements. Evidence from the passage may include quotations, but these should be supported by explanations. *Approach to marking shown in the 'Additional Guidance' column. Key differences and similarities shown in the grid below. Other answers are possible.*	5	The mark for this question should reflect the quality of response in two areas: • Identification of the key differences and similarities in attitude/ideas. • Level of detail given in support. The following guidelines should be used: • **5 marks** – comprehensive identification of three or more key differences and similarities with full use of supporting evidence. • **4 marks** – clear identification of three or more key differences and similarities with use of relevant supporting evidence. • **3 marks** – identification of three or more key differences and similarities with supporting evidence. • **2 marks** – identification of two key differences and similarities with supporting evidence. • **1 mark** – identification of one difference or similarity with supporting evidence. • **0 marks** – failure to identify any key difference or similarity and/or total misunderstanding of task.

Key differences	Tom Chivers	David Adam
Pieces of research that begin articles are diametrically opposed on effect of meat-based diet on health.	Opens by discussing recent research suggesting meat is harmful. Evidence in the study in *Cell Metabolism* suggested meat-eaters had shorter lives. Meat-eating caused cancer. Meat-eating as dangerous as smoking.	Looks at recent research suggesting healthiest diet is meat-based. Loren Cordain, nutritionist at Colorado University, claims it helps people lose weight and even treats some diseases. Claims that our stone age ancestors survived as hunter-gatherers eating meat. Claims meat-based diet of people in Papua New Guinea stops them getting heart disease.
Key similarities	**Tom Chivers**	**David Adam**
Both writers accept that human metabolism is complicated.	'the body is very complex'.	'If only things were that simple'.
Both note that nutritionists disagree.	Reference to 'red wine and chocolate' suddenly being called healthy. Disagreement over 'safe' allowances of sugar. Some say risks of saturated fats have been exaggerated.	Reference to nutritionists disagreeing over dropping food groups; Toni Steer disagrees with 'paleo' diet since it requires this. Archaeologists believe stone age diet varied from place to place – there was no one diet.
Conclusions both suggest balanced approach and reject extreme theories.	'None of these studies is the final truth'. Best advice is what mother told you.	Stone age diet was more mixed than Cordain believes.

PRACTICE PAPER 2

Dogs (pages 85–88)

Question	Expected response	Maximum mark	Additional Guidance
1. a)	Candidates should identify any **two** reasons why the writer was inclined to take the dog. Candidates must use their own words. No marks are awarded for verbatim quotations from the passage. *Possible answers shown in the 'Additional Guidance' column.*	2	• It was a cold, dark, cheerless time of year in late January and it would cheer her up. • It was a miserable time of year with bad weather and it would help cheer her up. • The writer needed cheering up since she felt oppressed by bills, being on a diet and filling in tax forms. • She was susceptible to hard luck stories and the pup had been rejected. • The fact the pup had been rejected as a Christmas present made her feel sorry for it.
1. b)	Candidates should refer to at least two features of language in lines 4–7, and analyse how the writer uses these to convey her feelings for the dog. Marks will depend on the quality of comment. 2 marks may be awarded for a reference to a language feature plus detailed/insightful comment; 1 mark for reference plus more basic comment; 0 marks for reference alone. Marks can be awarded as 2+2, 2+1+1 or 1+1+1+1. *Possible answers shown in the 'Additional Guidance' column.*	4	**Sentence structure:** • Minor sentence: 'A small male … ten weeks old' provides a list of the pathetic features of the dog, which are appealing as it is so young and small. • 'Eyes like chocolate buttons…' is a minor sentence with a short list of similes describing the lovable appearance of the dog. **Word choice:** • 'all wobbly and scared' – comical description shows vulnerability of dog, which appealed to her. • 'love at first sight' – cliché has humorous effect; hyperbole tells how she adored it from the start. • 'teeming with fleas' is horrible, and contrasts with the cuteness of the dog. **Imagery:** • 'Eyes like chocolate buttons': image appeals to taste, provides picture of big brown eyes, just like the sweets, as if dog was good enough to eat, showing she loved its looks. • 'fur as soft as pussy willow': pussy willows are velvety in texture – image effectively evokes soft tactile texture of dog's fur, which suggests her affection for it. • 'malodorous as a goat': goats are proverbially smelly, and this simile is humorous as she loved the dog despite this.

Question	Expected response	Maximum mark	Additional Guidance
			Contrast: • 'one perfectly excellent dog': contrasts with all the drawbacks of the 'rampaging puppy'. This makes her love for the puppy comical. • 'love at first sight': contrasts with 'sheer madness', admitting she adored the dog despite its faults. **Tone:** • Tongue-in-cheek tone of 'It was love at first sight' is very humorously placed after the negative comments on the smell and fleas. • 'It was also sheer madness': hyperbole has humorous tone as she admits taking the dog was unwise.
2.	Candidates should provide a brief summary of **two** of the reasons. Candidates must use their own words. No marks are awarded for verbatim quotations from the passage. *Possible answers shown in the 'Additional Guidance' column.*	2	• She knew she was being foolish. • The family already had a very nice dog. • The writer worked full time and had two children to look after. • Their house was rather small, and certainly did not have enough room to enable a lively puppy to run about. • She knows if she had thought out the consequences she would probably not have taken it.
3.	Candidates should refer to at least **two** features of language, and analyse how the writer uses these to convey the characteristics of the dog. Marks will depend on the quality of comment. 2 marks may be awarded for a reference to a language feature plus detailed/insightful comment; 1 mark for reference plus more basic comment; 0 marks for reference alone. Marks can be awarded as 2+2, 2+1+1 or 1+1+1+1. *Possible answers shown in the 'Additional Guidance' column.*	4	**Sentence structure:** • Short topic sentence: 'all puppies are, by definition, cute' has amusing, mock serious tone. • Sentence 'Bichons are … adorability' is a list of amusing images, leading to the climax of the last one. • Repetition of 'adorable' stresses this feature: 'It's not just…' **Word choice:** • 'sultans of soppy': calling a tiny fluffy dog a 'sultan' is comic as the image is of a grand middle-eastern chief. • Use of list of superlatives: 'sweetest … sunniest … kindest … most patient' emphasises they have an excellent temperament. **Imagery:** • 'kings of cute': suggests an image of the dog as leader in a kingdom of cute dogs as it was so appealing. • 'sultans of soppy': alliteration enhances the image of the dog as a Turkish chief in a kingdom of appealingly vulnerable dogs. The image is very humorous. • 'Olympic champions of adorability': image humorously suggests cuteness could become an Olympic sport, and if so, her dog would be the winner.

Question	Expected response	Maximum mark	Additional Guidance
			Tone: • Humorous tone in 'even traffic wardens are nice to you', as people think of traffic wardens as very severe. • Humorous, fond tone of 'the space between those fluffy ears of theirs' is effective in making the dog seem lovable, if not very clever. • Comic and indulgent tone in description of dog dressed up as a fairy in the doll's pram shows it has a lovely temperament.
4.	Candidates should refer to at least **two** features of language, and show how these help convey the problems she faces with the dog in a humorous way. Marks will depend on the quality of comment. 2 marks may be awarded for a reference to a language feature plus detailed/insightful comment; 1 mark for reference plus more basic comment; 0 marks for reference alone. Marks can be awarded as 2+2, 2+1+1 or 1+1+1+1. *Possible answers shown in the 'Additional Guidance' column.*	4	**Sentence structure:** • Use of ellipsis after 'Marlon Brando' is effective in delaying the absurd idea of the macho actor trapped in the 'body of a teddy bear'. • Listing of dog's childlike characteristics, 'very jolly, very affectionate', in the sentence 'owning a bichon…' sets up a humorous tone. **Word choice:** • Use of archaism in 'woe betide us' has a humorous effect. • 'a skilful combination of anguish and resentment' is comic as these emotions are quite subtle, sophisticated and very human, suggesting the dog is quite manipulative, although it is just a young puppy. • Comparison to 'a dirty sheepskin rug' is highly humorous, particularly after all the details about washing and trimming. **Imagery:** • 'like having a very jolly … toddler': comparing the dog to a baby is a funny image, suggesting it is also lovable but requiring constant attention. • 'the body of an overgrown teddy bear' is an endearing image as it compares the dog to a much-loved children's soft toy. **Tone:** • Tongue-in-cheek tone: suggesting the dog might be 'the reincarnation of some great actor' is a very ridiculous hyperbole. • 'I picture Marlon Brando trapped … teddy-bear': the tone here is tongue-in-cheek as neither a small fluffy puppy nor a teddy bear is anything like Marlon Brando, an actor known for being macho, sullen and moody. • Comparison with Lady Gaga – making her look 'low maintenance' is very humorous as the singer is known for outrageously complicated outfits. The contrast with a tiny dog is very funny.

Question	Expected response	Maximum mark	Additional Guidance
5. a)	Candidates should identify any **three** of the behaviour problems the writer had to face with her dog. Candidates must use their own words. No marks are awarded for verbatim quotations from the passage. *Possible answers shown in the 'Additional Guidance column.*	3	• The dog would not stay in a dog bed, but insisted on sleeping in the writer's bed, sometimes on top of her head. • If the writer tried to keep the dog out of her bedroom he would keep hurling himself at the door in frustration. • At first the dog would try and jump on her back while she was driving. • The dog refused to use the dog flap in the door despite great efforts to teach him, but kept scraping the door instead. • The dog destroys many things by chewing them, particularly shoes. • The dog is very greedy and will eat all sorts of unsuitable things, sometimes making himself sick.
5. b)	Candidates should analyse how the writer uses sentence structure effectively to convey the behaviour problems. At least two examples must be discussed for 4 marks. Marks will depend on the quality of comment. 2 marks may be awarded for a reference to a sentence structure feature plus detailed/insightful comment; 1 mark for reference plus more basic comment; 0 marks for reference alone. Marks can be awarded as 2+2, 2+1+1 or 1+1+1+1. *Possible answers shown in the 'Additional Guidance' column.*	4	• Use of a question followed by the answer: 'Can I get him … expense? Can I hell.' Repetition of 'can' and this structure emphasises writer's frustration. • Use of a list without the word 'and' ('toothbrushes … post') emphasises the number and variety of things the dog destroys. • Use of short sentences and informal language followed by parenthesis has humorous effect in 'You name it … chew it to death'. This helps convey her frustration at the dog's destructiveness. • The parenthesis – 'and the most financially disastrous' – helps emphasise the cost of the dog chewing up expensive shoes.
6.	Candidates should evaluate the final paragraph's effectiveness as a conclusion to the passage as a whole. Marks will depend on the quality of comment. For full marks there must be appropriate attention to the idea of a conclusion. A more basic comment may be awarded 1 mark. *Possible answers shown in the 'Additional Guidance' column.*	2	• The first sentence undercuts the previous catalogue of bad behaviour and damage to sum up very economically why they put up with the dog. • The simplicity and conversational tone of the first sentence is quite moving. • The description of the 'bichon blitz' and the language of 'chasing a mad white furball round the park' follow up on the humorous tone used throughout the rest of the passage. • The final sentence is particularly effective as it sums up the dog's nature with an aphoristic and euphonious phrase: 'incorrigible but thoroughly irresistible'.

Question	Expected response	Maximum mark	Additional Guidance
7.	Candidates should identify key areas of disagreement in the two passages by referring in detail to both passages. There may be some overlap among the areas of disagreement. Markers will have to judge the extent to which a candidate has covered two points or one. Candidates can use bullet points in this final question, or write a number of linked statements. Evidence from the passage may include quotations, but these should be supported by explanations. *Approach to marking shown in the 'Additional Guidance' column.* *Key areas of disagreement are shown in the grid below. Other answers are possible.*	5	The mark for this question should reflect the quality of response in two areas: • Identification of the key areas of disagreement in attitude/ideas. • Level of detail given in support. The following guidelines should be used: • **5 marks** – comprehensive identification of three or more key areas of disagreement with full use of supporting evidence. • **4 marks** – clear identification of three or more key areas of disagreement with use of relevant supporting evidence. • **3 marks** – identification of three or more key areas of disagreement with supporting evidence. • **2 marks** – identification of two key areas of disagreement with supporting evidence. • **1 mark** – identification of one key area of disagreement with supporting evidence. • **0 marks** – failure to identify any key area of disagreement and/or total misunderstanding of task.

Areas of disagreement	Sarah Vine	Grant Feller
Feelings towards dogs in general.	Loves dogs – 'we love him'; has owned (at least) two dogs, and is sad one is now dead. Prepared to put up with problems like fleas and smell.	Hates dogs, and admits this even though he knows it will make people dislike him. Loathes dogs for being 'smelly, waste-producing', etc.
Idea of dogs being 'cute' and loveable.	Believes puppies are 'by definition' cute; alludes to 'chocolate button eyes' and 'fur as soft as pussy willow'.	Is unmoved by dogs who are 'fluffy, doe-eyed, saliva-sharing', etc.
Sense that everyone is friendly when you have a puppy with you.	'even traffic wardens are nice to you' when you are walking a bichon.	Very unhappy about encounter with a playful dog on a beach in Cornwall that knocked over his son, and with the friend who brought a dog to his barbecue and proceeded to let it run amok and eat the expensive sausages bought for his guests.
Idea that dogs are charming and to be treated like children.	Refers fondly to her dog being dressed as a fairy and wheeled in a doll's pram.	Very disdainful of guest carrying the 'coochie-poochie-woochie' in her arms. The language mocks the baby talk he despises.
Regarding a dog as if it were human.	Talks of her dog as if he were human: compares him to Marlon Brando; sees him as reincarnation of an actor; attributes human emotions such as anguish and resentment to him.	Disapproves of the way they have become 'extensions of our human selves' according to their 'deluded owners'.

Areas of disagreement	Sarah Vine	Grant Feller
Attitude to dogs charging around in public places.	She admits her dog goes wild in the park and rushes about 'like a loon'; chasing it makes her really happy.	He disapproves, and uses ironic tone to mock attitude of indulgent dog owners; 'what's wrong with them barking', etc.
Attitude to dogs' behaviour.	She sees it as just its nature to behave like this: 'that's bichons for you'.	Resents this attitude: 'they're just expressing themselves!', exclamation mark shows his exasperation with this.

PRACTICE PAPER 3

Old Age (pages 89–92)

Question	Expected response	Maximum mark	Additional Guidance
1. a)	Candidates should explain what is involved in the 'game' the writer invites the reader to play. Candidates must use their own words. No marks are awarded for verbatim quotations from the passage. *Possible answers shown in the 'Additional Guidance' column.*	2	Any two of: • Select an old person whom you do not know. • Study him or her carefully. • Try to guess the person's age.
1. b)	Candidates should analyse how the writer's use of language emphasises society's negative view of old people. Marks will depend on the quality of comment. 2 marks may be awarded for a reference to a language feature plus detailed/ insightful comment; 1 mark for reference plus more basic comment; 0 marks for reference alone. Marks can be awarded as 2+2, 2+1+1 or 1+1+1+1. *Possible answers shown in the 'Additional Guidance' column.*	4	Possible answers include: • 'Crusty': slang, derogatory tone, lack of respect. • 'Contagious': connotations of disease. • Emphasis on physical weakness and decline – 'wrinkles', etc.; connotations of words such as 'sunken', 'frail', 'damp', 'sagging'. • Listing of such features stresses sense of decay. • Imagery of 'eroded' and 'archipelagos' – comparison with features of landscape suggesting natural process of decay.
2.	Candidates should identify what the author believes the 'game' will demonstrate. *Possible answers shown in the 'Additional Guidance' column.*	2	Two separate points for 1 mark each: • That younger people cannot distinguish between elderly people of different ages. • People do not want to face up to old age.
3.	Candidates should refer to at least **two** features of language, and analyse how the writer conveys people's fear of old age. Marks will depend on the quality of comment. 2 marks may be awarded for a reference to a language feature plus detailed/insightful comment; 1 mark for reference plus more basic comment; 0 marks for reference alone. Marks can be awarded as 2+2, 2+1+1 or 1+1+1+1. *Possible answers shown in the 'Additional Guidance' column.*	4	• Use of emotive terms such as 'terror' and 'horror'. • Use of first person plural and words like 'collective' emphasise how fear of the elderly is endemic. • Connotations of 'consign' – e.g. normally applies to objects rather than people; inhuman desire to send the elderly away. • Imagery of 'netherworld' – comparison to underworld or hell; elderly left to suffer in a place where others need not see them. • Hyperbolic imagery of 'zombies' and 'horror movies' – implication that the elderly are like the 'living dead'.

Question	Expected response	Maximum mark	Additional Guidance
4.	Candidates should identify the differences between attitudes to old people in Western countries and other parts of the world such as Africa. Candidates must use their own words. No marks are awarded for verbatim quotations from the passage. Marks can be awarded as 2+2, 2+1+1 or 1+1+1+1. *Possible answers shown in the 'Additional Guidance' column.*	4	Possible answers for 1 mark each include: **Other cultures such as Africa:** • Old cared for in family unit or in neighbourhood. • Old given respect because of their age. • Old valued because of their knowledge and perception. **Western countries:** • People desperately try to delay the ageing process. • People use any strategy (dieting, psychology, etc.) they think will help. • People dress to look younger and resort to cosmetic surgery.
5. a)	Candidates should identify what the writer considers to be the 'greatest shame and horror of our society and our age' for 2 marks. Candidates must use their own words. No marks are awarded for verbatim quotations from the passage.	2	Paraphrase of 'Most people in this country die weepingly lonely – cold, starved, and left in no doubt that they have overstayed their welcome' (e.g. Most elderly people die alone in a state of physical and emotional distress).
5. b)	Candidates should analyse how the writer's word choice conveys the strength of his feelings about this. Marks will depend on the quality of comment. 2 marks may be awarded for a reference to a language feature plus detailed/insightful comment; 1 mark for reference plus more basic comment; 0 marks for reference alone. Full 3 marks can be gained by 1+1+1 or 2+1 according to quality of comment. *Possible answers shown in the 'Additional Guidance' column.*	3	Comment on the connotations of the emotive language used, e.g. • 'consign' – impersonal word usually used of goods • 'banish' – conveys sense of rejection and finality • 'weepingly' – emotional suffering • 'lonely' – sense of isolation • 'cold'/'starved' – physical discomfort; people deprived of basics of life • 'unwelcome' – old people are unwanted.
6.	Candidates should evaluate the final paragraph's effectiveness as a conclusion to the passage as a whole. Marks will depend on the quality of comment. For full marks there must be appropriate attention to the idea of a conclusion. A more basic comment may be awarded 1 or 2 marks. Marks can be awarded as 2+2, 2+1+1 or 1+1+1+1. *Possible answers shown in the 'Additional Guidance' column.*	4	• Summarises the key message of the passage by ending with a plea for everyone to take an interest in the lonely old people known to them. • Repeated use of first person plural stresses the concern, seen throughout the passage, that this is an issue that affects everyone. • Second sentence summarises the two themes developed earlier in the passage: (a) people fear growing old, and (b) this fear can only be overcome by taking an interest in the old. • Short final sentence states the point in an even more abbreviated form for impact. • Last sentence has a balanced structure (antithesis) to show that there is a benefit to both parties in doing this.

Question	Expected response	Maximum mark	Additional Guidance
7.	Candidates should identify key areas of disagreement in the two passages by referring in detail to both passages. There may be some overlap among the areas of disagreement. Markers will have to judge the extent to which a candidate has covered two points or one. Candidates can use bullet points in this final question, or write a number of linked statements. Evidence from the passage may include quotations, but these should be supported by explanations. *Approach to marking shown in the 'Additional Guidance' column. Key areas of disagreement are shown in the grid below. Other answers are possible.*	5	The mark for this question should reflect the quality of response in two areas: • Identification of the key areas of disagreement in attitude/ideas. • Level of detail given in support. The following guidelines should be used: • **5 marks** – comprehensive identification of three or more key areas of disagreement with full use of supporting evidence. • **4 marks** – clear identification of three or more key areas of disagreement with use of relevant supporting evidence. • **3 marks** – identification of three or more key areas of disagreement with supporting evidence. • **2 marks** – identification of two key areas of disagreement with supporting evidence. • **1 mark** – identification of one key area of disagreement with supporting evidence. • **0 marks** – failure to identify any key area of disagreement and/or total misunderstanding of task.

Areas of disagreement	A.A. Gill	Lonnette Harrell
Passage 1 concentrates on negative aspects of old age while passage 2 highlights the positives.	Emphasis on physical decay ('wrinkles', 'sunken cheeks', etc.); loneliness; health problems, etc. Defines old age as an absence of youth, interest, choices, etc.	Sees old age as a time to find joy in living; a time to try new things, etc. Emphasises the new choices on offer – mentoring the young, etc.
Passage 1 is directed at those who are not old; Passage 2 concentrates on the activities and state of mind of the elderly themselves.	Argues that our treatment of the elderly reveals our own fear of the ageing process. 'Can you tell me how old they actually are?' 'We treat the old so badly...'	Examples of positive pursuits: developing new relationships; cultivating the spiritual dimension of life; desire to make the most of remaining time.
Passage 1 has a polemical dimension; passage 2 aims to describe the opportunities of old age.	Condemns people for lack of concern for the elderly: 'It's you and I who have the problem'; 'You don't look because you don't care'.	Gives examples of people who have been more productive in their senior years; other examples of positive activities and attitudes referred to above.
Passages offer contrasting explanations for the problems of the elderly.	Passage 1 sees society's treatment of old people as the reason for their isolation (i.e. external factors).	Passage 2 sees the individual's outlook as the key to happiness in old age (i.e. internal factors).
Passages offer contrasting solutions to the problems of the elderly.	Asks other age groups to change their attitude to the elderly. Solution lies with others, who must 'include the old in our lives' and value their experience and entertaining stories.	Suggests that the elderly can improve their lives through adopting a positive approach. 'Nothing external can give you the peace and calmness that comes from inner joy.'

PRACTICE PAPER 4

Cycling (pages 93–95)

Question	Expected response	Maximum mark	Additional Guidance
1.	Candidates should identify the attitude taken in The Netherlands towards cycling for 1 mark. Candidates must use their own words. No marks are awarded for verbatim quotations from the passage. Candidates should analyse how the writer's use of imagery helps the reader to understand this attitude. Marks will depend on the quality of comment. 2 marks may be awarded for a reference to an image plus detailed/insightful comment; 1 mark for reference plus more basic comment; 0 marks for reference alone. *Possible answers shown in the 'Additional Guidance' column.*	3	Cycling is highly regarded, treated with respect and admiration, even veneration/awe. • The writer comments that 'cycling is taken more seriously than any religion' and this reference is developed through various religious images. • Answers should identify and comment on at least one of the religious images, e.g.: 'Nirvana': refers to a state of bliss and inner peace to which the Buddhist aspires. 'Promised Land': refers to the land promised to Abraham by God in the Bible. 'Mecca': regarded as the holiest city in Islam, to which Muslims are required to make a pilgrimage. • Each reference implies a place to which the believer wishes to go or a state of mind he or she wishes to achieve. • Similarly, cyclists regard The Netherlands as a place of great significance/perfection and long to go there.
2.	Candidates should identify any **four** aspects of cycling in The Netherlands that differ from Scotland. 1 mark for each point. *Possible answers shown in the 'Additional Guidance' column.*	4	Any four separate points, such as: • In The Netherlands most people ride a bicycle each day. • It is the norm for children to cycle to school. • It is the law for shops to have cycle racks outside. • Politicians have to take cyclists' opinions seriously. • All new roads have clearly defined cycle lanes. • The land is flat, meaning expensive features on bicycles like lightweight frames or multiple gears are unnecessary.

Question	Expected response	Maximum mark	Additional Guidance
3.	Candidates should refer to at least **two** features of language and analyse how the writer conveys the difficulties of being a cyclist in Scotland. Marks will depend on the quality of comment. 2 marks may be awarded for a reference to a language feature plus detailed/insightful comment; 1 mark for reference plus more basic comment; 0 marks for reference alone. Full 3 marks can be gained by 1+1+1 or 2+1 according to quality of comment. *Possible answers shown in the 'Additional Guidance' column.*	3	• In Scotland the landscape is much more hilly. Tone of 'Steamroller the Cairngorms' humorously conveys the impossibility of adopting the kind of cycling associated with The Netherlands. • The weather is more severe in Scotland. Imagery of 'never-ending battle' conveys the idea that the cyclist has to fight constantly against the elements. • Balanced sentence structure of 'if the hills don't do you in, the wind probably will' shows it is impossible to avoid one or other of these problems. • 'Stoicism' is a philosophy that implies self-control and perseverance in the face of difficulty; writer suggests that such an attitude is necessary for a cycling enthusiast in the Scottish climate. • 'fundamentalist mind': suggests the necessity of an unshakeable, unquestioning belief in the rightness of your cause. • 'Promised Land': determination, vision and faith are required in order to overcome the obstacles. • 'cross an eight-lane motorway thundering with juggernauts': hyperbole emphasises the many physical challenges involved.
4. a)	Candidates should explain the writer's personal opinion of cycling enthusiasts. *Possible answers shown in the 'Additional Guidance' column.*	2	Cynical, sarcastic, dismissive or mocking **(1 mark)** because he believes they take cycling too seriously or are too zealous, etc. **(1 mark)**.
4. b)	By referring to at least two examples, show how his use of word choice and/or imagery helps to convey this opinion. Marks will depend on the quality of comment. 2 marks may be awarded for each reference plus detailed/insightful comment; 1 mark for reference plus more basic comment; 0 marks for reference alone. Marks can be awarded as 2+2, 2+1+1 or 1+1+1+1. *Possible answers shown in the 'Additional Guidance' column.*	4	Two of the following: • 'fanatics': a fanatic is someone who is full of excessive zeal for his cause; suggests cyclists are too single-minded in their obsession. • 'a wee moan': informal, colloquial register suggests writer thinks that cyclists are constantly complaining; minimises the importance of what they see as major problems. • 'permanent sense of grievance': believes they consider themselves to be unfairly discriminated against. • 'exude righteousness': mocks their sense of moral superiority as they believe they are 'saving the planet'. • 'chirrup': image compares their complaints to noises made by a bird; implies a non-stop stream of complaints, again mocking/trivialising the cyclists' opinions.

Question	Expected response	Maximum mark	Additional Guidance
5.	Candidates should identify **three** criticisms the writer makes of the behaviour of cyclists on the roads. Candidates must use their own words. No marks are awarded for verbatim quotations from the passage. *Possible answers shown in the 'Additional Guidance' column.*	3	Any three of the following for 1 mark each: • 'cyclists hunt in packs': they group together rather than going in single file. • They do not use the cycle lanes that they say they want. • They hold up traffic on country roads by failing to ride in single file. • They deliberately ride in this way in order to antagonise motorists ('goad').
6.	Candidates should first identify the two specific measures that should be taken to regulate cyclists. Candidates should then explain what the writer considers to be the advantages of these. Candidates must use their own words. No marks are awarded for verbatim quotations from the passage. *Possible answers shown in the 'Additional Guidance' column.*	4	Two measures are: bicycles should have number plates **(1 mark)** and cyclists should pay a licence fee **(1 mark)**. Advantages: • Number plates would make it easier to deal with cyclists who do not stick to the rules **(1 mark)**. • A licence fee would mean that, as cyclists were making a contribution in return for using the roads, they would be entitled to make their complaints heard **(1 mark)**.
7.	Candidates should evaluate the final paragraph's effectiveness as a conclusion to the passage as a whole. Marks will depend on the quality of comment. For full marks there must be appropriate attention to the idea of a conclusion. A more basic comment may be awarded 1 mark. *Possible answers shown in the 'Additional Guidance' column.*	2	Any two points such as the following: • Use of puns: 'high ground' and 'low gears' refer back to 'bumpy parts of Scotland' to create humour. • Effectiveness of humour of comparing literal and metaphorical ('moral high ground' can 'only be reached in … low gears'), given that the subject matter concerns cycling. • Use of minor sentence at the end gives greater impact to the point. • Tone of mockery used earlier is sustained in the last paragraph.
8.	Candidates should identify key areas of agreement/disagreement in the two passages by referring in detail to both passages. There may be some overlap among the areas of agreement/disagreement. Markers will have to judge the extent to which a candidate has covered two points or one. Candidates can use bullet points in this final question, or write a number of linked statements. Evidence from the passage may include quotations, but these should be supported by explanations. *Approach to marking shown in the 'Additional Guidance' column.* *Key areas of disagreement are shown in the grid below. Other answers are possible.*	5	The mark for this question should reflect the quality of response in two areas: • Identification of the key areas of agreement/disagreement in attitude/ideas. • Level of detail given in support. The following guidelines should be used: • **5 marks** – comprehensive identification of three or more key areas of disagreement with full use of supporting evidence. • **4 marks** – clear identification of three or more key areas of disagreement with use of relevant supporting evidence. • **3 marks** – identification of three or more key areas of disagreement with supporting evidence. • **2 marks** – identification of two key areas of disagreement with supporting evidence. • **1 mark** – identification of one key area of disagreement with supporting evidence. • **0 marks** – failure to identify any key area of disagreement and/or total misunderstanding of task.

Areas of agreement and disagreement	Alan Taylor	Susan Swarbrick
Both writers portray cyclists as obsessively dedicated to their interest.	Use of religious imagery.	Similar idea in 'unwavering devotion'. Words like 'habit' and 'addiction' imply a comparison to drugs.
Both writers stress the physical demands of cycling.	'cycling in Scotland is not for the faint-hearted'; challenges of weather and hilly landscapes.	References to wind, rain and hills in paragraph 2.
Passage 1 focuses on negative aspects; passage 2 sees these aspects as positives.	Points out disadvantages of Scotland compared to The Netherlands with regard to cycling.	Sees the difficulties as challenges to be enjoyed; 'I loved every second'.
Passage 1 views cycling from the point of view of a non-participant; passage 2 is from the perspective of a cycling enthusiast.	Discusses problems caused by cyclists for other road users, especially when they are in groups.	Sees a beauty in groups of cyclists on the roads: 'few sights are more enthralling than … a professional peloton in full flight'.
Contrasting opinions on the personalities and attitudes of cyclists: Passage 1 sees cyclists collectively as self-righteous and complaining; passage 2 highlights the camaraderie and shared values.	'strained stoicism'; 'wee moan'; 'permanent sense of grievance', etc.	'gentleman's rules', 'old-fashioned etiquette'.
Passage 1 mocks cyclists for taking themselves too seriously; passage 2 reveals a capacity for self-mockery.	'fundamentalist mind'; 'not for the faint-hearted', etc.	'As addictions go, admittedly it is spiralling'; she watched 'not the highlights, the whole shebang'; 'whimsical romanticism'; 'geek', etc.

APPENDIX I

GRAMMAR AND SYNTAX

SENTENCES, CLAUSES AND PHRASES (PAGE 98)

Analyse the following sentences and fill in the table.

a) *I told the children a story.*
b) *The light shone into the room.*
c) *The aircraft crashed just after take-off.*
d) *She found the missing money in the tea caddy.*

Subject	Verb	Indirect object	Direct object	Adverbial phrase
I	told	the children	a story.	
The light	shone			into the room.
The aircraft	crashed			just after take-off.
She	found		the missing money	in the tea caddy.

WORD ORDER: INVERSION (PAGE 99)

Consider what effect is obtained in the following examples of inversion.

a) (i) His fist smacked down on to the table.

   (ii) *Down smacked his fist on to the table.*

     In example (ii), placing the stressed word 'Down' at the beginning of the sentence has the effect of onomatopoeia because of the 'd' sound; it imitates the thud of the fist on the wood. In the normal word order (i), 'His', a less-heavily-stressed, softer-sounding word, begins the sentence. This does not have the same effect.

b) (i) The car door opened and the Queen stepped out.

   (ii) *The car door opened and out stepped the Queen.*

     In sentence (ii), placing the subject at the very end of the second clause of the sentence creates a climax. The reader is kept waiting to find out who stepped out of the car and is surprised to learn it is the Queen. In the normal word order of sentence (i), this suspense and surprise is lacking.

c) (i) A beautiful princess lived in a dark and gloomy castle in the middle of a dense forest.

   (ii) *In the middle of a dense forest, in a dark and gloomy castle, lived a beautiful princess.*

     Sentence (ii), in which the verb and subject are delayed until the end after a number of phrases, is typical of story-telling. The listener is kept in suspense before finding out who lives in the place that is gradually described. Suspense keeps the reader enthralled.

d) (i) I have never done that.

   (ii) *That, I have never done.*

     In example (ii), stress is thrown on to the word 'That'. It makes whatever it refers to sound extremely important and serious. When 'that' is placed last, as in example (i), it is relatively unstressed. The action itself assumes much less importance.

e) (i) For Henry Jekyll stood there before my eyes, pale and shaken, and half fainting and groping before him with his hands like a man restored from death!

   (ii) *For there before my eyes – pale and shaken, and half fainting, and groping before him with his hands like a man restored from death – there stood Henry Jekyll!*

     Example (ii) is the original quotation from R.L. Stevenson's *The Strange Case of Dr Jekyll and Mr Hyde*. It is similar in structure to example (c), above. By keeping the main verb and subject until the end of the sentence, aided by an effective use of the dash, which delays the end of the sentence further, Stevenson creates a most thrilling climax. The identity of the person follows a list of intriguing descriptive phrases that keeps the reader guessing who is being described until the dramatic disclosure at the end of the sentence.

ACTIVE OR PASSIVE? (PAGE 100)

1. *Change the following sentences from active to passive voice:*
   a) *The guard overpowered the prisoner.*
      The prisoner was overpowered by the guard.

   b) *The cat caught the mouse.*
      The mouse was caught by the cat.

2. *Now change these sentences from passive to active voice:*
   a) *The sculpture was made by Michelangelo.*
      Michelangelo made the sculpture.

   b) *Norway was invaded by the Germans.*
      The Germans invaded Norway.

SENTENCE STRUCTURE (PAGES 104–105)

Comment on the authors' use of sentence structure and consider their purpose in the techniques they have chosen.

1. The word 'action' at the end of the first sentence is followed by a series of sentences containing verbs of action, all following the subject 'he'. The progression of energy expressed by the verbs indicates the character's pent-up frustration: 'took', 'tossed', 'pulled', 'flung', etc. The repetition of 'and' also heightens the sense of restlessness and activity.
   The extract also shows a good use of personification in the first sentence. The simile 'crouched … like a depressed relation' adds a touch of black humour and shows how the character finds his surroundings dreary and oppressive.

2. Repetition is used effectively in starting the first two sentences in the same way: 'Ivy is…' This is followed by a list of descriptive noun phrases summing up the evil nature of the plant. The lists each build to a climax as the phrases get longer and more complex and the characteristics more absurdly over-the-top. The next three sentences adopt a similar technique, but, after saying what ivy *is*, the writer now uses lists of verb phrases describing what ivy *does*. Making ivy the subject of the first five sentences ascribes a tongue-in-cheek sense of importance to the ivy, as if a spotlight is on the plant. The subjects of the next three sentences are the victims of ivy: three different types of plant. Personification is the dominant figure of speech as the writer imagines ivy to be a barbarian warrior violently attacking the innocent occupants of gardens.
   Extremely emotive and violent language is used to humorous effect: 'smothers', 'throttled', 'crushed', etc. This is humorous as plants move very slowly and imperceptibly, while these words suggest sudden movement. He attributes human characteristics to the victim plants (a technique known as anthropomorphism), using words like 'gallant' and 'blameless', which is also amusing. Apart from the absurdity of the personification, he shows he is not serious by using colloquialisms like 'bossy-boots'.

3. This extract makes clear use of inversion: 'Back we went', 'down we went'. These emphasise the impression of the characters retracing their steps to look for the lost brooch.
   The frequency of the participles – 'searching', 'following', 'refinding', 'pushing' – reinforces the sense of urgency in the search.

4. The repeated use of the passive voice – 'was told', 'it was alleged', 'he was said', 'the alarm was raised' – is typical of the impersonal, objective tone of legal proceedings.
   It should be noted how this cool tone contrasts with the violence of the subject matter: 'threatened with a knife'.

5. This narrative is written in the historic present tense: 'feels', 'has'. This lends a heightened sense of drama and immediacy to the story. In the penultimate sentence there is a series of participial phrases (based on the participles 'littering', 'unfolding' and 'shaking'), which stresses the prolonged nature of the search for the money. The final sentence is a short, bald statement. It gives the appearance of an anti-climax, and in a sense it is, but it actually raises the tension as the search has been in vain. The simplicity of the language makes it all the more hard-hitting.

6. The most noticeable feature of this extract is the extreme length of the sentences. The second one seems interminable, with a long series of rambling phrases beginning with 'from'. One would expect finally a phrase beginning with 'to' to complete the idea of a range of experiences, but this never arrives. The effect is incoherent and formless.

The word choice is equally opaque. The list of extremes and superlatives – 'extraordinary', 'boundless', 'incredible', 'greatest', 'endless', etc. – becomes tedious and absurd and ultimately fails to have any effect. There are several grandiloquent phrases that actually mean very little: 'authentic cultural matrix', 'refined facets', etc. The use of imagery is also unselective and overdone. The extended image – 'tesserae of the wonderful mosaic' – is actually quite appropriate in describing the beauty spots that comprise the Sorrento coast. It suggests many beautiful pieces making up a wonderful whole, and mosaic is a typically Italian art form. The writer then gets bogged down in an excess of metaphors that are much less well chosen, however. Describing the perfume of the flowers as a 'jewel' is not a helpful comparison, nor is the 'disturbing voice of silence'.

In this piece of writing the writer is striving much too hard for effect, and in being unselective he becomes almost incomprehensible. That it is a translation may in part account for the stylistic flaws.

PRACTICE PAPER

TIGER MOTHER (PAGES 60–61 AND 106)

Question	Expected response	Maximum mark	Additional Guidance
1. a)	Candidates should explain in their own words the meaning of the opening sentence. A paraphrase of 'nothing is fun until you're good at it' is required. *Possible answer shown in the 'Additional Guidance' column.*	2	Chinese parents understand that children won't enjoy an activity until they have worked hard enough to master it.
1. b)	Candidates should refer to at least five of the stages in the 'virtuous cycle'. Candidates must use their own words. No marks are awarded for verbatim quotations from the passage. *Possible answers shown in the 'Additional Guidance' column.*	5	1 mark each for any five of the following: • Children are always initially reluctant to work. • The parent must override this reluctance and force them to work and practise. • Practice and repetition gradually enable children to perform very well. • After they have begun to do well they get praised for their achievements and start to find it rewarding. • The praise and satisfaction gives them confidence in what they are doing and makes the activity enjoyable. • This change in attitude makes it easy for the parent to persuade the children to work even harder.
1. c)	Candidates should analyse how **one** language feature conveys the meaning effectively. Marks will depend on the quality of comment.	2	**Sentence structure:** • Repetition of 'good at' in first two sentences mimics the progression towards excellence being described. • Repetition of 'practice, practice, practice' mimics the process by which Chinese children are forced to learn. • Repetition of 'this' at the opening of the last two sentences stresses the idea of progression to a goal. **Word choice:** • 'fortitude' is effective in expressing the bravery and stamina parents must have in order to drive their children to succeed.

Question	Expected response	Maximum mark	Additional Guidance
	2 marks may be awarded for a reference to a language feature plus detailed/insightful comment; 1 mark for reference plus more basic comment; 0 marks for reference alone. *Possible answers shown in the 'Additional Guidance' column.*		**Imagery:** • 'a virtuous circle': metaphor is by analogy with the more common 'vicious circle', which describes a chain reaction spiralling downwards. The 'virtuous circle' shows a successful progression upwards **Contrast:** • 'Chinese parents' are contrasted with 'Western parents'. Chua shows her awareness that the Chinese approach is very different to that accepted in most Western countries. **Tone:** • 'Tenacious practice, practice practice…': use of repetition creates forceful, persistent tone, illustrating the technique she is advocating.
2.	Candidates should explain how each anecdote illustrates the different attitudes to parenting. Up to 2 marks may be awarded for a clear explanation of each anecdote for a total of 4 marks. *Possible answers shown in the 'Additional Guidance' column.*	4	• The first anecdote describes how her father insulted her by calling her 'garbage' when she had been rude to her mother. His tough discipline made her feel ashamed of her behaviour and taught her a valuable lesson. It illustrates how Chinese parents are not afraid to use harsh discipline in the way they bring up their children. • The second anecdote tells of how guests at a dinner party were very shocked when she confessed to having called her own daughter 'garbage' after she had been rude to her. One guest could not even stay in the same room afterwards. This illustrates the American attitude to discipline, which is to avoid doing or saying anything that they feel might upset their child and damage their confidence.
3.	Candidates should identify linking function in argument. 1 mark will be awarded for quoting a reference to the topic previously discussed and summarising it briefly; 1 mark will be awarded for quoting a reference to the new topic being introduced and summarising it briefly. *Possible answers shown in the 'Additional Guidance' column.*	2	'How Chinese parents get away with what they do' refers back to her examples of the harsh discipline meted out to children by Chinese parents (including herself). The 'three big differences' between the Chinese and Western parental mind-sets refers to the way in which the Chinese approach to parenting is different to the Western way. These differences account for how they 'get away with it' without damaging or antagonising their children, and she will go on to describe and explain them in the next part of the passage.

Question	Expected response	Maximum mark	Additional Guidance
4. a)	Candidates should identify the **three** differences described in lines 27–57 between Chinese and Western attitudes to parenting. Candidates must use their own words. No marks are awarded for verbatim quotations from the passage. *Possible answers shown in the 'Additional Guidance' column.*	3	• Chinese parents are less concerned about their children's self-esteem and will punish them if they don't do as well as expected, while American parents are so worried about upsetting their children they will praise them even if they have performed poorly. • Chinese parents believe their children owe them for their upbringing and should repay them by performing well. American parents have the attitude that children do not ask to be born and so it is up to the parents to make their (unasked for) lives as good as possible. • Chinese parents believe they know best and impose their wishes on their children. American children expect their parents to wait on them.
4. b)	Candidates should refer to at least **two** features of language, and analyse how the writer uses them to convey the Chinese attitude to parenting. Marks will depend on the quality of comment. 2 marks may be awarded for a reference to a language feature plus detailed/insightful comment; 1 mark for reference plus more basic comment; 0 marks for reference alone. Marks can be awarded as 2+2, 2+1+1 or 1+1+1+1. *Possible answers shown in the 'Additional Guidance' column.*	4	**Sentence structure:** • The short sentence 'Chinese parents aren't' contrasts with the longer, more complex sentences describing Western parental angst that precede it. The shortness reflects the simple, no-nonsense Chinese approach. • 'tutoring, training, interrogating and spying': long list of present participles conveys the amount of energy that parents put in; meanings become more extreme showing parents adopt quite an antagonistic attitude to achieve the results they want. • Repetition of 'can't' in line 54 – 'Chinese daughters can't … camp' – illustrates repressive, authoritarian attitude. **Word choice:** • 'gasp in horror': hyperbole of reaction shows how seriously Chinese parents treat lack of success. • 'Chinese parents demand': verb 'demand' illustrates authoritarian attitude. • 'excoriate, punish and shame the child': list of strongly emotive verbs stresses the severe way in which Chinese parents treat their children. **Imagery:** • 'sacrificed': image has religious connotations and suggests extreme seriousness of Chinese parents' attitude. They will renounce things that are important in their own lives to advance their children. • 'Chinese mothers get in the trenches': image suggests Chinese mothers treat education like a war, and are prepared to suffer to be successful.

Question	Expected response	Maximum mark	Additional Guidance
			Contrast: • 'they assume strength, not fragility': contrast stresses how much Chinese parents expect of their children and why they do not hold back from punishing them. **Tone:** • Confident, assertive tone in presenting Chinese parenting methods. Many sentences begin in a similar, decisive way: 'The Chinese mother will… Chinese parents demand… the Chinese parent believes…', etc. • 'God help any Chinese kid…': tone is almost apprehensive, as if Chinese parental discipline is something to be feared.
5.	Candidates should evaluate the final paragraph's effectiveness as a conclusion to the passage as a whole. Marks will depend on the quality of comment. For full marks there must be appropriate attention to the idea of a conclusion. More basic comments may be awarded 1 or 2 marks. *Possible answers shown in the 'Additional Guidance' column.*	3	• 'Don't get me wrong': has a humble, pleading tone, as if she wants readers to be on her side. This contrasts effectively with her earlier, more assertive tone when she was outlining examples of the strict discipline and study regimes that Chinese parents could 'get away with' and criticising the Western approach as feeble. • 'It's not that Chinese parents don't care': she makes a plea that the apparently harsh regime has a loving basis. This repeats her earlier assertion that 'plenty of ego-inflating parental praise' is 'lavished' on the children in private, and that parents devote long hours to helping them. • 'Just … children': she uses two short simple sentences (the first a minor sentence), worded simply. This simplicity creates a tone of sincerity that emphasises her point that the 'tiger mother' just does what she thinks is best for her children. • 'just an entirely different parenting model': acknowledges that there are different approaches to parenting, which may both be right. This softens the harshness of her earlier, more dogmatic tone, which seemed to imply that Western parents' methods were ineffective, and only Chinese methods were right. She ends the passage on a suitably conciliatory note.
6.	Candidates should identify key differences and similarities in the two passages by referring in detail to both passages. There may be some overlap among the differences and similarities. Markers will have to judge the extent to which a candidate has covered two points or one. Candidates can use bullet points in this final question, or write a number of linked statements.	5	The mark for this question should reflect the quality of response in two areas: • Identification of the key differences and similarities in attitude/ideas. • Level of detail given in support. The following guidelines should be used: • **5 marks** – comprehensive identification of three or more key differences and similarities with full use of supporting evidence. • **4 marks** – clear identification of three or more key differences and similarities with use of relevant supporting evidence.

Question	Expected response	Maximum mark	Additional Guidance
	Evidence from the passage may include quotations, but these should be supported by explanations. *Approach to marking shown in the 'Additional Guidance' column. Key differences and similarities shown in the grid below. Other answers are possible.*		• **3 marks** – identification of three or more key differences and similarities with supporting evidence. • **2 marks** – identification of two key differences and similarities with supporting evidence. • **1 mark** – identification of one difference or similarity with supporting evidence. • **0 marks** – failure to identify any key difference or similarity and/or total misunderstanding of task.

Key differences	Amy Chua	Jemima Lewis
• How strict the writer is as a parent. • How much effort/ sacrifice the parent makes. • Degree to which children should be pushed. • How hard children should be driven.	• Chua admits to being very strict and forcing her children to work hard. • Chua's effort is so extreme it requires 'fortitude'; she says parents like her 'would give up anything' to help their children. • Believes that children are resilient and respond well to being pushed to become high achievers. • Chua approves of children being made to work hard and practise repeatedly.	• Lewis has a more relaxed attitude. She lets her children watch too much television, for example. • Lewis admits to 'lazy' parenting, and being 'too tired and busy' to take them to activities which would add to their 'accomplishments'. • Her mocking tone in 'ferrying children between Mandarin lessons and taekwondo' suggests she disapproves of pushing children too hard. • Lewis does not force her children to 'practise piano scales until their fingers throb'. Her tone in 'barking out instructions' is negative.
Key similarities	**Amy Chua**	**Jemima Lewis**
• Belief that you should make an effort in bringing up your children. • Belief that 'pushy' parents are not the evil tyrants portrayed by some critics. • Belief that pushing children is actually evidence of love.	• Chua thinks Western parents give up too easily. • Chua describes being 'ostracised' at a dinner-party when she described how strict she was with her children. She was herself brought up in this strict way by her own parents and she believes it did her good. She clearly respects her own parents, and does not regard them as monsters. She sees this strict method of bringing up children as just 'a different parenting model'. • Chua maintains Chinese parents care about their children: 'they would give up anything for their children'.	• Lewis admits she is a rather lazy parent when it comes to nurturing her children's 'accomplishments' which suggests she believes she should make more of an effort. • Lewis mocks the 'boo hiss' attitude of the critics (Blom and Robinson) to over-zealous parents and thinks it wrong to class them with parents who neglect and abuse their children. She satirises their critical attitude to pushy parents: 'gimlet-eyed Lady Macbeth of the nursery', showing she regards it as exaggerated. The reason she does not criticise such 'pushy parents' is that she sees the whole picture – they are 'actual people', not 'fairy-tale villains'. • Lewis accepts that pushing children to achieve is a form of love: the 'over-excited father … may be embarrassing, but at least he is there.' Spending time driving children to classes and extra-curricular activities is 'an expression of love'.